LEADERSHIP
is
Common
Sense

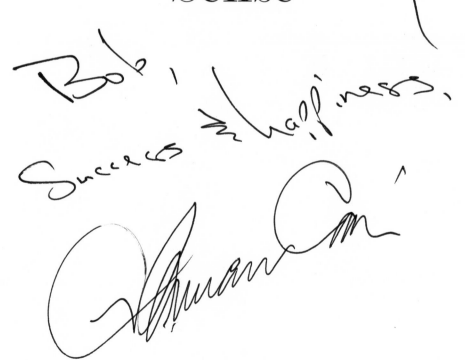

Bob,

Success & happiness,

LEADERSHIP
is
Common
Sense

Herman Cain

Chairman and CEO, Godfather's Pizza, Inc.
"The Hermanator"™

Foreword by Jack Kemp

VAN NOSTRAND REINHOLD
I⟨T⟩P® A Division of International Thomson Publishing Inc.

New York • Albany • Bonn • Boston • Detroit • London • Madrid • Melbourne
Mexico City • Paris • San Francisco • Singapore • Tokyo • Toronto

Van Nostrand Reinhold Staff:

Publisher: Melissa A. Rosati
Project Devevelopment Editor: Joan Petrokofsky
Assistant Editor: Amy Beth Shipper
Editorial Assistant: Jill Elias
Marketing Manager: Mary Fitzgerald

Marketing Assistant: Michelle Agosta
Senior Production Editor: Jacqueline A. Martin
Production Manager: Louise Kurtz
Production Assistant: Carolyn Holfelder
Designer: Paul Costello

I(T)P® an International Thomson Publishing Company
The ITP logo is a registered trademark used herein under license

Printed in the United States of America

For more information, contact:

Van Nostrand Reinhold
115 Fifth Avenue
New York, NY 10003

Chapman & Hall GmbH
Pappelallee 3
69469 Weinheim
Germany

Chapman & Hall
2-6 Boundary Row
London
SE1 8HN
United Kingdom

International Thomson Publishing Asia
221 Henderson Road #05-10
Henderson Building
Singapore 0315

Thomas Nelson Australia
102 Dodds Street
South Melbourne, 3205
Victoria, Australia

International Thomson Publishing Japan
Hirakawacho Kyowa Building, 3F
2-2-1 Hirakawacho
Chiyoda-ku, 102 Tokyo
Japan

Nelson Canada
1120 Birchmount Road
Scarborough, Ontario
Canada M1K 5G4

International Thomson Editores
Seneca 53
Col. Polanco
11560 Mexico D.F. Mexico

1   2   3   4   5   6   7   8   9   10   QEB-FF   01   00   99   98   97   96

Library of Congress Cataloging-in-Publication Data

Cain, Herman.
    Leadership is common sense / by Herman Cain.
        p. cm.
    Includes bibliographical references and index.
    ISBN 0-442-02368-5
    1. Leadership. I. Title.
HD57.7.C35   1996   96-31822
658.4'092—dc20   CIP

http://www.vnr.com
product discounts • free email newsletters
software demos • online resources

email: info@vnr.com

A service of I(T)P®

"THE HERMANATOR"

Around the time we were working with Herman Cain on health care reform and other National Restaurant Association issues in 1994, I stumbled across the movie "The Terminator" while cable grazing.

One of my favorite lines from the movie is Arnold Schwarzenegger's guttural catch phrase "I'll be back," an especially appropriate line for a character who was impossible to stop and kept popping up everywhere.

At the time, Herman was receiving very heavy press coverage for his "debate" with President Clinton on health care and appearing all over the country on a variety of issues.

Herman was impossible to stop and kept popping up everywhere. Hence, "The Hermanator."

As the final proof of how appropriate the nickname is, I ran the Microsoft Word spell-checker on this memo. It did not recognize the word "Hermanator." The spell-checker listed one possible alternative — "Terminator."

LARRY MCCARTHY
Partner
Gannon, McCarthy & Mason, Ltd.

CONTENTS

FOREWORD

BY JACK KEMP

During the eight months I worked side-by-side with Herman Cain, whom I invited (and Senator Bob Dole and Speaker Newt Gingrich had appointed) to serve on the National Commission for Economic Growth and Tax Reform, I came to see many sides of the man I would come to know as my friend.

I listened as the mathematician by training grilled our economists on the more esoteric aspects of tax reform, and then as the shrewd businessman, demanded an accounting of how proposals would impact small businesses. I watched the preacher in him emerge as he passionately argued for a "head start" for those at the bottom of the economic ladder. I tried, more than once, to gavel our hearings to order after Herman's mischievous wit had buried us in laughter. And finally lifted my glass when, during our farewell dinner, he rose to serenade fellow commissioners with the poetry of Rudyard Kipling.

This is why I was somewhat surprised by the title of his book, *Leadership Is Common Sense*. There is nothing "common," in the sense of "ordinary," about Herman Cain or the path he traveled to entrepreneurial success and national prominence. But as I turned the pages of his book, and with them the chapters of his life, I began to realize the sense he had intended.

Leadership is the ability to liberate potential, whether that potential resides in a business, an economy, a people, or within the human heart. To use Herman's metaphor, leadership is the gift of grasping that "seed of corn," and cultivating it to the fullest harvest. Or of using his determination to "work a little harder and work a little longer" (not to mention dream a little bigger and risk a little bolder) to fashion extraordinary achievement out of ordinary circumstance.

Even so, the "ordinary" experience of growing up in the segregated South is one many Americans today can hardly imagine. Despite having endured the cruelty of *de jure* Jim Crow laws and *de facto* racism, it says something poignant about the spirit of a man who covers these painful memories in a few paragraphs, and then fills a book with the story of a life that rose above them.

This is but one similarity between the story of Herman Cain and that of another African American who bulldozed racial barriers and blazed a trail of leadership that Americans of every color were drawn to follow. General Colin Powell, through a combination of grit, talent, and valor rose rapidly through the ranks of the United States military to become one of the most revered warriors and charismatic figures of our time. Not only did he pioneer new territory for African Americans, his example helped reaffirm our faith in America.

Herman Cain is the Colin Powell of American capitalism. His conquests won't be counted in terms of countries liberated or lives saved, but in those things that make life worth living—expanding opportunity, creating jobs, and broadening horizons, not just for those he knows, but through his example, for those he'll never meet.

Like Powell, Herman Cain is a man with a code—a moral template which binds together all the diverse experiences in his book. Every story—from learning to play the trombone to his leveraged buyout of Godfather's Pizza—illustrates a moral principle. In this sense, his telling becomes a living "Book of Virtues," in which we can discern the organizing patterns of his life, and draw lessons for our own.

It is not surprising that two men of such deeply felt conviction should find themselves in the spotlight of national politics. Powell, by all accounts, is an unwilling politician. And Herman Cain might be described as an accidental one.

When a local television station invited Herman Cain to participate in a televised "Town Hall" meeting with President Bill Clinton over health care reform, he certainly didn't *plan* on stumping the President or crystallizing public concerns about the administration's plans. He only wanted to ask a question: What should I say to those employees your plan will force me to fire? The by now legendary confrontation that ensued has been credited as the Waterloo of the Clinton Administration's campaign to nationalize health care.

Working together on the National Commission for Economic Growth and Tax Reform, holding cross-country hearings on problems with the current tax system, and shaping the outlines of a single-rate system to replace it, I came to appreciate the debating skills I had first witnessed in that prime time encounter. And in the end, as I watched Herman tame a lion's den of reporters, speak with the farmers, and small businesspeople he had helped organize in Omaha, and browbeat, reason, and cajole critics over to our point of view, I would be thankful to have Herman Cain on our side. It was the first, but I doubt the last, of the fights we would be leading together. And, as anyone who reads the pages can only conclude, Herman Cain's "American Journey" is just the beginning.

JACK KEMP
Vice-Presidential Candidate (1996)

INTRODUCTION

I have been "accused" of being a leader ever since I ran for student body president in the 7th grade. At that time I had barely learned how to spell leadership, so I certainly had little understanding of what leadership was or what makes a leader.

Most of my career I have been encouraged to take leadership positions without consciously pausing to reflect upon "why" I was encouraged to lead, or "what" I was supposed to do as "the leader."

After graduating from Morehouse College in 1967 and starting my professional career, I realized that businesses paid "mo money" to people who could really lead and get results ("leadership") versus someone who just occupied a position, which a colleague of mine calls "positionship."

"Mo money" was a motivator for me early in life because my family did not have a lot of money when I was growing up. As my career progressed I became more and more motivated by increased responsibility, challenging objectives, and the "thrill of victory" when I achieved goals beyond expectations. I was even more motivated when I achieved results that were not expected to be achieved at all.

I have held a wide range and variety of leadership positions (see Appendix A). This does not make me an expert, but it does give me enough battle scars to have an experiential perspective on what causes people to respond positively and effectively to a leader. People always want to feel that you genuinely listen to what they say, even if you decide not to pursue their idea. People want to feel they contribute to something successful, and that you as leader appreciate their contribution even if no one else understood their impact. People want to be led by leaders they admire and trust, and most people want to respect their leaders even if they do not like them. If people *do* like their leader, then it's a bonus.

I believe *great leaders are born* and *good leaders are made.* What better example of a born great leader than one of the most admired and respected presidents in our history, Abraham Lincoln. I do not recall ever reading that Lincoln took a leadership seminar. And even more amazing, "Lincoln was viewed by his own advisors as nothing more than a gawky, second-rate country lawyer with no leadership experience" (Phillips 1992). Maybe someone forgot to tell Lincoln that he was not supposed to succeed at reuniting the United States of America, and that he was not supposed to sign the Emancipation Proclamation. Great leaders instinctively possess and demonstrate the qualities and abilities discussed in this book, whereas good leaders have to work at them.

I do believe that all of us possess some leadership and that we can become good leaders. Just as some of us must work harder to learn how to sing, some of us have to work harder at becoming a good leader. As Bob Windham, a good friend, reminded me one day while we were playing golf and discussing a different subject, "We have to save the savable." When I lost that seventh grade election I was disappointed, and wondered if that was the end of my career as a leader. Fortunately, I ran for student body president again my senior year in high school and won. So, if you are "savable," keep trying, and this book should help.

Despite all the books and articles written and published on the subject of leadership there still appears to be a severe *deficiency* of good leadership in many organizations and institutions. Just examine the number of failed businesses annually, a staggering waste of human capital.

Business failures, out-of-control governmental budget deficits, or social organizations constantly struggling to survive, make it easy to conclude that there is room for one more good book on leadership. Well, here it is!

The difference with this leadership book, however, is that my career represents *success against many odds*, achieved with a person-to-person leadership style. Leadership is dynamic and continuous, rather than static and discrete. If you wait for a "leadership moment" to lead then it could be too late. This book focuses on the "three plus three" critical components of leadership which are easy to remember and easy to apply every day. Eventually, "Three Plus Three" becomes "common sense."

"Three plus three" refers to the *three critical qualities* a leader must possess, and the *three critical things* a leader must do. This idea evolved from a great number of speeches I have given on the subject of leadership, where I was compelled to distill my ideas on the subject into 30 to 45 minutes. Most people do not want to listen to even a *good* speech for more than 30 minutes, and citing more than three key points in a speech for the audience to remember is oratorical disaster. But more importantly, these critical components of leadership have always been at the heart of the leadership challenges that I have been able to successfully conquer.

This book is not presumed to be a cure-all for all leadership woes. This is a guidebook, not a textbook. Chapter 1 presents the "three plus three" principles and the basis for my audacious assertion that something as complex as leadership can be described with a simplistic concept. Chapter 2 is the story of how I climbed the "corporate ladder" at The Pillsbury Company and Burger King Corporation, and the leadership challenges I faced along the way. Chapter 3 is the unpredictable story of my ten years at Godfather's Pizza, Inc., and how these principles effected a "turnaround" situation and the subsequent purchase of the company. Chapter 4 is the unplanned and unlikely nationally televised incident between President Clinton and me on the subject of his national health care proposal. Some observers described this incident as the turning point of the 1994 national health care debate. Chapter 5 is an illustration that *success has been a journey and not a destination* through the first 50 years of my life, and Chapter 6 is my perspective on leading your life to live *your* dreams.

The proliferation of social and community organizations which are well intended but struggling to survive is a missed opportunity for more effectively providing assistance for human needs problems. And the waste and inefficiency in many, but not all, sectors of government is simply pathetic. This book is based on experiences, observations, and lessons learned from *my journey*, and by sharing them, I hope that more people and organizations will "succeed" more often.

HERMAN CAIN
Fall 1996

ACKNOWLEDGMENTS

My sincere thanks to:

God for this life and "journey."

My family (Gloria, Melanie, and Vincent) for always being there.

The following people for their assistance in research and reviewing the manuscript: Kathy Woodall, Kathleen Sullivan, Dennis Pierson, Ron Gartlan, and Gary Batenhorst.

Melissa Rosati and VNR for taking the chance on an unknown "writer."

Everyone who has touched my life with inspiration and unforgettable experiences.

LEADERSHIP
is
Common
Sense

"THREE PLUS THREE" LEADERSHIP

Three Critical Qualities a Leader *Must* Possess

THE D-FACTOR
Happiness

THE E-FACTOR
Risk Index

THE F-FACTOR
Lost and Found

Three Critical Things a Leader *Must* Do

IDENTIFY AND REMOVE BARRIERS
Wrong Job
Right Job

LEAD
The Right Questions
Get Ugly

INSPIRE

LIVE YOUR DREAMS

It must be borne in mind that the tragedy *of life does not lie in not reaching your* goals, *the tragedy lies in not having any goals to reach.*

It isn't a calamity *to die with* dreams *unfulfilled, but it is a calamity not to dream.*

It is not a disaster *to be unable to capture your* ideals, *but it is a disaster to have no ideals to capture.*

It is not a disgrace *not to reach the* stars, *but it is a disgrace to have no stars to reach.*

Dr. Benjamin E. Mays

When life and times were simpler, we could explain many complex phenomena with concepts as simple as "one plus one" or "two plus two." In today's technologically fast-paced and dynamic world, it requires "three plus three" descriptions to begin to come close to representing the complex as simple. Leadership is certainly complex.

Studies on leadership identify and analyze numerous leadership characteristics and duties, but few leave the reader with a concise working model which can be used daily in the midst of a problem, or in the face of challenging leadership decisions. Concepts, principles, instructions, or values which are internalized can be applied spontaneously and repeatedly. Soon they become like *common sense.* When a building is on fire, that's not the time to look in the fire drill manual to learn how to fight the fire. However, just as exceptional proficiency in any skill or art requires proficiency in the fundamentals and practice, good leadership requires proficiency in the fundamentals and a lot of practice.

The three critical qualities a leader must possess and the three critical things a leader must do are fundamental. A leader must have the ability to recognize that people must motivate themselves, the ability to take risks and make the tough decisions, and the ability to block out the unnecessary in a situation and concentrate on the necessary. I call these the D, E, and F factors—the world might appreciate the D, E, and F of something instead of another A, B, and C of everything. The three critical things a leader must do are *remove* barriers to motivation, *lead* the actions required to achieve the desired results, and *inspire* the passion within people to perform better than expected. These principles are shown in Exhibit 1-1 for quick reference.

Exhibit 1-1   *"Three Plus Three" Leadership*

Three critical qualities a leader must possess:

D-Factor (Drucker)	Ability to recognize that people must motivate themselves
E-Factor (Entrepreneurial)	Ability to take risks and make the tough decisions
F-Factor (Focus)	Ability to block out the unnecessary and concentrate on the necessary

plus

Three critical things a leader must do:

REMOVE	the barriers which prevent people from being self-motivated
LEAD	the actions required to achieve desired results
INSPIRE	the passion within people to perform better than expected

—The Hermanator

To test my audacious assertion that leadership can be described in these "three plus three" critical components, I examined a study by Kouzes and Posner which ranks 20 leadership characteristics of most admired leaders. Their results, based on 1987 and 1983 surveys, show that the top four characteristics remained the same—honesty, forward-looking ability, inspirational talents, and competency (Exhibit 1-2).

Interestingly, three of the repeat top four characteristics showed a measurable change of nine percentage points from the 1987 survey

Exhibit 1-2 *Characteristics of Admired Leaders*

Characteristic	1993 U.S. Respondents Percentage of People Selecting	1987 U.S. Respondents Percentage of People Selecting
Honest	87	83
Forward-looking	71	62
Inspiring	68	58
Competent	58	67
Fair-minded	49	40
Supportive	46	32
Broad-minded	41	37
Intelligent	38	43
Straightforward	34	34
Courageous	33	27
Dependable	32	32
Cooperative	30	25
Imaginative	28	34
Caring	27	26
Mature	14	23
Determined	13	20
Ambitious	10	21
Loyal	10	11
Self-controlled	5	13
Independent	5	10

Kouzes and Posner, Credibility

to the 1993 survey. My interpretation of this trend is that *people have an even greater anxiety about the need for honest, visionary, inspiring, and fair-minded leaders* to deal effectively with the vast number of social, economic, and political challenges of our times. Even more interesting is that the desire for leaders to be "competent" decreased nine points, whereas the other three increased by nine points, which

Exhibit 1-3 *A Comparison of "Three Plus Three" Leadership Principles and Characteristics of Admired Leaders*

I	II	III
D-Factor	**E-Factor**	**F-Factor**
Determined	Forward-looking	Straightforward
Ambitious	Broad-minded	
Self-controlled	Imaginative	
	Independent	
IV	V	VI
REMOVE Barriers	**LEAD Actions**	**INSPIRE People**
Competent	Courageous	Honest
Intelligent		Inspiring
Mature		Fair-minded
		Supportive
		Dependable
		Cooperative
		Caring
		Loyal

could signal an increasing recognition that *leaders are not required to have all the answers.* Rather, people want leaders to be able to inspire the best in others, not just give orders and commands.

Using a common sense interpretation of each characteristic identified in the study, I mapped the 20 characteristics to the "three plus three" principles to see if there was a logical correlation, especially since many people use different words to describe the same leadership characteristics. This produced the relationships between the Kouzes and Posner characteristics and the "three plus three" principles shown in Exhibit 1-3.

First, it is interesting that eight of Kouzes and Posner's characteristics relate to the ability to inspire, and four relate the entrepreneurial ability of a leader. This suggests eight qualities which are naturally inspiring to people and four different adjectives to describe that critical entrepreneurial E-factor. It also suggests a strong bias about *what people want most from an admired leader,* namely someone who can ignite the "fire in the belly" (inspire) and is willing to take risks *(E-factor)* even if this is not a character trait of their own.

Second, the D-factor (self-motivated) and the leadership duty to remove barriers to motivation relate to three each of the Kouzes and Posner characteristics. This suggests that *although self-motivation and the ability to identify and remove barriers to motivation are important, they are not as looked for as the "risk-taking" and "inspiring" characteristics of leadership.*

Third, I find it odd that the *"focus" and "lead"* duties received only one Kouzes/Posner characteristic each, since I would consider these two principles most important if I were forced to reduce "three plus three" to "one plus one." This could signal that *these qualities are hardest to find in leaders,* and most often hardest to articulate by those looking for leadership. This would support the fact that only a few people are truly good leaders, and for whatever reason, people do not consciously look for a leader to be focused and decisive as often as they look for them to be inspirational and entrepreneurial.

Overall, the exercise using Kouzes and Posner's results makes a strong statement about the audacious assumption that leadership can be described in "three plus three" terms. Although one could argue the validity of my interpretation of the 20 Kouzes and Posner characteristics, one would have to admit that the relationships are compelling. Let's elaborate on this model.

Three Critical Qualities a Leader *Must* Possess

THE D-FACTOR

During my employment with the Coca-Cola Company in the mid 1970s, I had the opportunity to attend a seminar where the well known management thinker Peter Drucker was a speaker. Although I have retained regrettably little from the numerous presentations I have attended on the subject of leadership over the years, I distinctly remember one thing Drucker said during this seminar. His comment about motivation shaped my attitude about leadership from that point on: *"You can't motivate people, you can only thwart their motivation because people motivate themselves."*

This principle, which I call the D-factor, has significantly impacted my relationships with people since the day I heard Drucker present it. But more importantly, I have experienced its truth over and over again in my work with people and organizations. The rest of the story is that even though you can't motivate people as a leader, you must identify and remove the barriers to self-motivation.

High self-motivation *(D-factor)* is not a characteristic that everyone possesses. This is why I consider it a *critical* quality for a leader because without it, and without being able to recognize it in other people, one cannot lead anybody anywhere.

I did not grow up with the feeling that I was a "born leader" or that I always had to be the leader. But I have always been results-oriented—with ambition and determination—which happen to be two of the Kouzes and Posner characteristics mapped to the D-factor. I do not know how or why some people are more ambitious, determined, or results-oriented than others, but I'm sure there is a study out there somewhere that tries to answer that question. My intent in writing this book is not to advance the "science" of leadership, but to advance the "art" of leadership.

At each major decision point in my life and career (see Chapter 5), my own motivation has come from a deep desire to exceed expectations and make a difference. In doing so, life has been fun and I have experienced the true "secret to success"—happiness. If you are happy doing what you are doing, you will be successful.

One of my career goals as a young man growing up in Atlanta was to become a corporate vice president. I believed at the time that such an achievement would bring with it financial success and comfort, and therefore I thought I would be happy. I was content for a while, but after I had been Pillsbury's Vice President of Systems for two and one-half years, and after leading the systems organization to achieve some aggressive objectives for the company, I became bored. I was not challenged. When I am not challenged, I am not happy.

It was at that time that I changed careers to work my way up the ladder at Pillsbury's Burger King subsidiary in order to rekindle my own motivation. The idea of becoming an operations vice president with the potential of becoming a company president for somebody, somewhere, doing something was a motivating thought. Why? It would exceed a whole lot of expectations and allow me to make a whole lot of difference.

Happiness

Self-motivation and happiness are almost synonymous. If you are already happy you are motivated to stay happy, and if you are unhappy you are motivated to get happy. Many people have experienced the feeling of happiness without being able to explain or define the feeling. The same is also true of unhappiness.

A person who claims to be unhappy typically has a personal barrier to motivation, lurking around with "bad attitude" near the top of the list. Happiness begins with a good attitude and with knowing what would really make you happy, but people can't always answer that question.

No one can make another person happy in the same sense that, as Peter Drucker stated, no one can motivate another person. *An individual must motivate "self" and an individual must make "self" happy.* But what would really make a person happy other than the usual instant answer, "to be rich"? There are many documented cases of unhappy rich people. I believe a key to happiness is to know it when you see it, and to see it in your mind. Then, be able to articulate your picture of happiness into words.

A few years ago I heard the minister of my church here in Omaha,

Rev. Dr. Nigel McPherson, use some thought-provoking words to define happiness: *"something to love, something to do, and something to hope for."* "Wow!" I thought to myself that Sunday morning when I first heard this definition. It makes so much sense and explains why I have felt a sense of happiness most of my life, although I did not know exactly why or how to articulate my sense of happiness. I have always been blessed with loved ones (my parents, my wife, our children, and some very close friends). I have always had something to do (school, work, career, more work, and even more work) and I was never without hope for something...a healthy family, the next promotion, or the next "adventure" in my life or career. But additionally, this definition gave me a vehicle to stir peoples' thinking who may be searching for happiness in their jobs and lives or who may be trying to eliminate a "bad attitude." If one of Reverend McPherson's "somethings" is missing, you have a happiness deficiency that only you can fill. A good leader will help the individual identify a deficiency by asking some probing, non-personal questions to stimulate self-analysis of the problem. Then he or she should offer encouragement. Ultimately, however, the individual must fill the happiness deficiency.

When I have spoken with people about the happiness in their lives—or the lack of it— I have found that many people feel unhappy most often because they cannot answer the question, "What do you hope for?" In some cases, there is the spiritual hope, but not a clear sense of daily, living hope. Time and time again I have met unhappy people who feel they are trapped in their jobs, trapped in their lives, and facing the future with little hope.

The national unemployment rate is approximately five percent, which means ninety-five percent of the American work force has something to do...jobs. The majority of working people has family or loved ones. But opinion polls point out that many Americans are dissatisfied with their lives or their jobs. They feel cut off from the American dream, when in fact all of us had more to start our lives with than our parents.

I believe that much of the general public's dissatisfaction comes from negative news, political rhetoric, and the false perception that somehow the government or someone else is responsible for making them happy. This creates a mass "bad attitude," which is a major barrier to happiness. Are you happy? Take the happiness test, you could find self-motivation.

Something to love, something to do, and something to hope for, but the greatest of these is hope.

THE E-FACTOR

Risk Index

There is a lot of truth to the old saying that the only things certain in life are death and taxes (and at the rate taxes are increasing, taxes may soon kill us before we die). That means everything else in life is risky. Leadership is especially risky because every time you make a decision you run the risk of being wrong, but you also run the risk of being right!

Different people are comfortable with different levels of "risk." Some people will bet all that they own on an idea or "hunch," while others would not bet one dime of their own money on a seemingly sure thing. People select different careers because of certain risks associated with various career choices, often pursuing choices that are consistent with their "risk index." (It seems logical that there should be such a thing as a "risk index" in the world of behavioral research, but since the objective of this book is the "art" of leadership rather than the "science" of leadership, I will use the term "risk index" in a relative sense.)

During a presentation to a group of college students, I was discussing some risks I had taken in my career that led to my "success." I was also speaking about the need to have big dreams and not to be afraid to go after those dreams. In the question & answer session following my presentation, a student asked me, "What if you have big dreams and you want to be very successful but you do not want to take any risks, what do you do?" I responded, "Become an accountant." That is not a slap at the accounting profession, but it is a profession of consistently applying an established set of rules to data, which can be (but is not always) a very low-risk profession. It can also be very rewarding—but it takes a longer time to get there. On the other hand, one needs a high quantitative aptitude to be successful in the accounting profession, with a low appetite for risk.

A leader must be comfortable with risk in order to make decisions. A leader must also be prepared to be wrong, but good leaders tend to make more correct decisions than wrong ones. To put this another way, there really is no such thing as a right or wrong decision, just different consequences for taking different actions. If the consequences are desired consequences, then it was a "right" decision.

No one enjoys the feeling of being wrong about anything, but some people dislike being wrong more than others. Consequently, they try to minimize the risk of being wrong by not making a decision. There is another old saying, "If you can't stand the heat, stay out of the kitchen." Leaders are in the "kitchen" all the time, taking risks.

Leadership requires taking risks. In decision making, it occurs after analyzing and evaluating a problem or opportunity, because then you must complete the decision-making process based on what's inside of you…"gut feel." People with a very low risk index are uncomfortable with making "gut calls" due largely to the fear of being wrong. People with a high risk index are comfortable with making such calls and are usually excited about having the responsibility. Good leaders then work to achieve the desired outcome by using all their creative energies and instincts to overcome obstacles along the way. In the event they are wrong, they are self-motivated enough (D-factor) to re-evaluate, re-group, learn from the experience, and then go on.

The entrepreneurial spirit (E-factor) in a person is not a reckless abandonment of logic or common sense, it is an intuitive and positive view of the world as "a glass half full" instead of "a glass half empty." The entrepreneurial ability in good leaders allows them to use their creative talents positively to eliminate obstacles to achieving the desired results of their decisions. Dr. Robert Schuller, pastor of the Crystal Cathedral Ministries in Garden Grove, California, calls it "possibility thinking." I call it the E-factor.

THE F-FACTOR

Lost and Found

My first formal exposure to the concept of *focus* occurred on my way to Omaha for the first time in my life. The Pillsbury Company (TPC) had appointed me President of Godfather's Pizza, Inc. (GPI), effective April 1, 1986. I had made plans to go to the NCAA Final Four basketball tournament in Dallas, Texas, long before being appointed president of GPI. So I went to the tournament, which happened to be the weekend directly preceeding my first day on the job as GPI's new president.

I flew from Philadelphia to Dallas for the weekend tournament and found a book in the overhead compartment where I was seated. I told the flight attendant that I found the book and I asked if she wanted to turn it in to lost and found. She looked at the book and saw it was brand new and that no one's name was written in it. It even had the sales receipt tucked inside the pages. But nowhere was the owner identified. The attendant said to me, "It's your book now. Keep it."

The book was entitled *Marketing Warfare* by Al Ries and Jack Trout. Since I was intrigued by the title, I started to read it from the beginning and continued until we landed in Dallas. While in Dallas, I was so interested in what the book had to say that before I boarded my flight to Omaha that Tuesday morning, April 1, I had finished it.

In the book, Ries and Trout discuss the concept of defensive marketing strategy when you are not the first, second, or even the third largest competitor. The first principle of this concept is to focus your resources, because a smaller competitor cannot afford to fight a larger competitor, neither on his turf nor on his terms. All the while I was reading *Marketing Warfare,* I was thinking of what my new boss, Jeff Campbell, had clearly described I would be faced with at GPI as its new president.

Although I believe that I have always been a "cut to the chase," "get to the heart," "what's the bottom line" kind of person, this was the first time I had ever read anything that discussed the concept of focus so explicitly. It had an especially strong impact on me since I was on my way to take over a company in decline. I had some ideas about how I would approach the situation at GPI because Jeff had already asked me to put together a "100-day plan of attack." But, when I accidently found the book, I found the theme behind what we needed to do to turn GPI around...I found *focus.*

People who know me know that I am a Christian believer. I believe God wanted me to find that book when I did because He wanted me to succeed at GPI. To the person who bought the book *Marketing Warfare* and left it on an airplane...thank you!

The ability to block out the unnecessary is the willingness to concentrate your resources for more impact, just as one can deliver a more forceful blow with a fist than with an open palm. But as Ries and Trout point out, "the essence of focus is sacrifice." Leaders who cannot bring themselves to give up the unnecessary for the sake of the necessary do not possess the critical leadership characteristic of focus.

Another way to describe the focus quality in a person is the ability to see the forest and not just the trees. Most people have a natural tendency to be concerned only about their little corner of the forest, but leaders can instinctively maintain a perspective of the forest while being sensitive to individual "trees."

In the context of a typical organization, the leader must balance the input and contributions of each functional area, while focusing on the right priorities, following up on planned executions, and managing through the unexpected, while guiding the entire organization. Simultaneously, the leader must make key decisions, identify and remove barriers, and inspire the individuals in the organization...all this and still keep the organization *focused.* Just as some people naturally have a higher or lower risk index in their E-factor, some people are naturally more detail-oriented than others, which makes it more difficult for them to not worry about each "tree in the forest."

The converse is not true. Just because you are naturally focused does not mean you are not good with details. *Focused* people can handle details yet not be uncomfortable with leaving the details to someone else while they are concentrating on the "forest."

Establishing focus as a leader is not just a matter of using the word, it is a matter of actions and convictions as well as words. Just like that old Negro spiritual, "Everybody talking about heaven ain't going there," not everyone who can spell focus will know how to focus themselves or their organization.

Three Critical Things a Leader *Must* Do

IDENTIFY AND REMOVE BARRIERS

The list of barriers to self-motivation is endless, but the most common obstacles can be classified as job-related, family-related, or personal—all of which can impact a person's sense of well-being and influence their job performance.

It is the leader's direct responsibility to identify and remove job-related barriers such as wrong job, poor communications, inadequate training, improper working facilities, and others shown in Exhibit 1-4. These are barriers that can keep a person from maintaining focus on their job—which prevents them from performing their best.

At the top of the list of job-related barriers (although they are not in any particular order) is "wrong job." This potential barrier is the

Exhibit 1-4 *Barriers*

Job-related:	
Wrong Job	Discrimination
Poor Communications	Feeling Unappreciated
Job Insecurity (Fear)	Feeling of Entitlement
Poor Performance	Feeling Underpaid
Low Challenge (Too Easy)	Personality Conflict
Second Job	Inadequate Training
Personal:	
Not "Happy"	Inflated Ego
Low Risk Index	Lazy
Low Self-confidence	Dull Person
Low Self-esteem	Bad Attitude
Family-related:	
Miserable Marriage	Death of a Loved One
Too Much Debt	Divorce
Problem Child	No Family
Problem Relative	Illness

most difficult to deal with because if the person is in the wrong job for whatever reason, then removing the barrier means removing the person from the job. If you do not have the right person for the right job to begin with, trying to eliminate other job-related barriers is like trying to drain the Atlantic Ocean with a teaspoon.

Another golden nugget about removing barriers that I learned from Peter Drucker is that if you have a "people" problem, then fix it immediately. There is obviously a compassionate way to achieve this, but procrastinating on the action—once you are convinced you have identified the person as the barrier to their own success—is not fair to the organization or to the individual.

Wrong Job

During my first restaurant-related job with Burger King Corporation (BKC), I was assigned to a restaurant in the Minneapolis region. After about two months of "basic training," I was promoted to Assistant Manager and two months later I was assigned as Manager of the restaurant.

As the newly appointed manager, I inherited three assistant managers who had worked with me during my training. Two of the assistants (Dan and Kevin) had been in the business for two or three years each, and they both had good performance reputations in operations. Even better, they were also well-liked by the rest of the crew, and our district manager thought highly of them. They were dependable, responsible, competent, and all those other things you hope and pray for in assistants.

Steve was a different story. He had been with Burger King for nearly five years, two more than Dan and Kevin, but he was not nearly as competent and he didn't seem to relate well to the crew. I immediately saw the warning signs of Steve being a performance problem. When Dan and Kevin suggested not scheduling Steve to work during our busiest periods I asked, "Why?" They reluctantly said the restaurant's performance would suffer. They had experienced this many times when Steve had been left to run the restaurant as the person in charge.

Although I heeded their advice, I was compelled to schedule Steve as the lone shift leader on some occasions. In order to observe his performance first-hand, I also scheduled times when Steve and I would be working together. When I had the opportunity to see Steve's performance for myself, I knew Kevin and Dan were right—Steve was not comfortable in his position as a restaurant manager and he appeared to not comprehend many of the basics that most managers pick up during basic training.

When I asked my district manager why no one had done anything about Steve's situation, he told me the company was trying to give him a chance to "come around." Approximately five years at the same performance level, I thought to myself, and he still had not "come around"? The cows could have come home, had calves, and gone back to pasture in this time. I later realized that the issue was more management's hesitancy to make the tough call than it was giving Steve more time. By not doing anything, Steve was allowed to flounder while Burger King's customers received inconsistent quality and service.

After experiencing this situation for a few months (I was still relatively new and I wanted to be certain my instincts were right about Steve), I suddenly received word that the company was assigning me to another post—that of Vice President and Regional General Manager for one of its ten regions. This had been a goal of mine ever since I had resigned my position as a Pillsbury Vice President—so I was elated with the news. But I also felt that I could not leave Steve's situation unresolved.

On my final day as the restaurant's manager, and after the usual crew farewells, I asked Steve to meet me that afternoon in the company's regional office. I can still distinctly recall the room where we met—because on that day I did what should have been done years before—I fired Steve. This was not the first time I had been forced to fire someone, but it was the first time that the person really had no idea what was about to happen to him.

Steve came into the room and said, "Hello." I asked him to please have a seat. I said, "Steve, there is no easy way to do this so I will get to the point. You have been working for Burger King for nearly five years and you have not progressed beyond the assistant manager level. By this time most people in your position have already advanced to the store manager level. I have also observed first-hand that you have a really tough time running a smooth shift and relating well to the crew, although I know you are trying the best you can. Steve, as my last official action as manager, I have to terminate your employment with BK due to insufficient performance."

Steve was obviously shocked and immediately expressed his concerns of not being able to take care of his wife, who I now learned was expecting their first child (talk about feeling like Darth Vader). He also felt embarrassed at the prospect of having to tell his family that he had been fired. He poured out his feelings while I listened quietly.

When Steve calmed down (although he did not get immediately defensive or angry, which is typical in such situations), I then said, "Let's talk about what happens from this point on." I started by asking him how he came into this job at Burger King in the first place. He said this had been the only job offer he had received after college. He stated he had planned to work at Burger King for only a year or two until he could get something he liked. But he had remained this long because he had become more and more dependent on the income he was receiving. His salary had been increasing even though his performance had not.

I then asked him about the kinds of things he really enjoyed doing. He indicated he had always had a passion for electronics, and that he enjoyed trying to repair old radios and TV sets. He had never had any formal training in this area, but it was something he enjoyed doing. I then asked if he had ever considered a career as a computer systems technician or engineer. He said he had not because, frankly, he did not know what one was. I explained that they install, maintain, and repair computers and computer-related equipment. I then suggested that he apply for a position with one of the large computer companies headquartered in the area and that I would be happy to help him make some contacts.

Steve was in the wrong job. After talking with him, it turned out that he did not like what he was doing because it was not something he looked forward to doing every day. This is not to say that one must love every task on their plate every day, but a person must strive toward improving the list of things they enjoy doing or boredom, unhappiness, and complacency may result.

Steve took my advice and he eventually landed a position as a systems technician with a major computer company. Several years later

I heard from him. Steve thanked me for the advice I had given him and he *thanked me for firing him!* Leaders don't often get that type of feedback after firing someone, but with that critical "wrong job" barrier out of his way, Steve was a happier and more productive person.

Having to terminate an employee is one of the most stressful and painfully uncomfortable tasks of being a leader, but when it has a happy ending, it's more than worth it. It all begins with communication, which leads to better understanding, which leads to happiness, which leads to success.

Right Job

Many leaders have experienced the joy of having the right person in the right job, which usually makes most of the other job-related barriers irrelevant. The right person in the right job often finds ways to resolve potential barriers on his/her own, and in some instances he/she just ignores petty barriers because he/she is too busy having fun doing his/her job.

Win Wallin is one of my leadership heroes. He is one of those great American business leaders who may never become a household name. Win was President and COO (Chief Operating Officer) of The Pillsbury Company when I started there in 1977, and he suggested that I go to work for Burger King if I ever wanted to be president of something.

Win's career at TPC with Bill Spoor (Chairman and CEO) was impressive, with nearly 20 successive years of compound earnings growth. Even more impressive was Win's record at Medtronic, Inc., when he later became Chairman and CEO. From 1985 to 1995, Medtronic posted a compound annual growth rate (CAGR) in sales of 16.7 percent, and a compound annual growth in net earnings of 22.7 percent. Earnings per share grew 24.3 percent (CAGR), with a ten year average return on equity of 21.6 percent. This is not bad for a guy whom the Pillsbury Board of Directors did not feel was the right person to succeed Bill Spoor as Chairman and CEO when Bill retired.

History has proved that Win was the right person for the right job (CEO) at Medtronic, Inc.

When I asked Win about his views on leadership, he responded in typical Win Wallin fashion, "I really had not thought about it." After he did think about it for a moment, he stated, among other points, "identify good, talented people and put them in positions they enjoy doing."

At first mention that I should give up my comfortable vice president's job and go to work for Burger King starting at the bottom, I wondered for a moment if Win was trying to get rid of me. Maybe he saw something in me that I did not realize, because it was some of the best advice I have ever been given. I have a job I love doing.

Although the leader must continually deal with job-related barriers, it is not his or her job to remove family-related or personal barriers to motivation. However, a leader can encourage the individual to deal with family and personal barriers in order to achieve a balance between work and family.

Family-related barriers are generally more difficult to remove than personal barriers. That's no surprise—you cannot change who you have for parents, siblings, relatives, and children. You can disown and ignore friends and acquaintances, but what about the uncle that embarrasses everybody at the family reunion, or the brother that's the source of most of the troubling phone calls from your mother? And of course, your children are yours for life. A child "gone wrong" can be a constant detraction to personal and professional focus, making it an awesome barrier.

Family and personal problems are barriers to motivation in the work place. These are always stressful and difficult barriers to handle, but ultimately their resolution belongs to the individual. The best advice a leader can give someone with family or personal problems is to get professional help!

When barriers are removed, people are happier; The fewer the barriers, the happier they are. This usually lasts until they start focusing on another barrier.

LEAD

To lead is to *define the right problem, ask the right questions, select the right alternative,* and *achieve the desired results.* To lead may seem an obvious leadership responsibility, but it is sometimes stalled by indecisiveness, procrastination, or not enough E-factor to take the risk of being responsible for the consequences. A leader must lead...initiate action, show commitment to the action, and manage the actions necessary to achieve the desired results.

During my early days at GPI, we were looking for every opportunity to stimulate our sagging sales. One member of the management team was in charge of developing our pizza delivery capability, which at that time was only about ten percent of our restaurant sales. The previous leadership of the company had been hesitant about committing more resources to developing our delivery business. It was an added operational complexity—it cost more than the dine-in and take-out portions of our business. Some were also concerned that a full-scale delivery program might cause too many of our existing customers to stay home and just call us to deliver the pizzas to them, which would be more costly. Although the test results had indicated that not all customers would stay home, home delivery was still a big leap of faith for many of our operators, both company and franchised.

Having come to GPI with the objective of being a "leadership" franchisor rather than a "dictating" franchisor, we made the decision to move forward with delivery rollout in all our company units where it was physically possible to do so. We developed training tools, guidelines for implementation, and marketing and promotional support materials to make the rollout as smooth as possible. It was not a requirement for franchisees to participate, and it still is not a legal requirement today. After evaluating all available analysis, "asking the right questions," and listening to my management team, my job as leader was to say, "Let's do it and let's do it right." This inspired an attitude within the company of making it work...and it did. Over time, pizza delivery has grown to approximately 25 percent of our business, making it a nice complement to our dine-in and carry-out business.

A leader must also lead when a situation calls for a demanding, critical completion time. Obviously, the leader cannot require seemingly unrealistic schedules all the time or people may get burned out. Also, if every request from the boss is a crisis, then pretty soon no one responds because it does not really mean anything. But there are times when the leader must set a demanding schedule. When it is required and the team understands and buys into the necessity for such a demanding schedule, the team will actually be inspired to help make it happen, even if it requires working long hours and even longer days.

The Right Questions

The most important step in solving a problem is making sure you are working on the right problem. This requires asking the right questions, a tendency of mine which comes from having spent the first half of my career as a corporate problem solver in one capacity or another.

When President Clinton positioned his health care proposal (see Chapter 4) as wanting to provide health insurance coverage for the "one out of ten Americans" that did not have coverage, it was a well-intended point of focus. But when I asked the question, "What do I tell all those people whose jobs I will have to eliminate?," it exposed the fact that his plan would help one group of people by taking jobs from another. This also presented the real possibility that the new problem would have been worse than the problem he was trying to solve. Metaphorically, when a bridge is flooded, you can either raise the bridge or lower the river. The first question should be...how deep is the river, because we might want to drain it.

Not all problems can be solved more than one way, but many problems have multiple solution approaches, or they can be subdivided into solvable components. But it begins with asking the right questions.

When I became President of GPI I asked my people during an operations meeting what we stood for in the minds of our customers (see Chapter 3). When I did not receive a convincing response, I then asked, "What did we used to stand for in the mind of the customer?" That question produced the hesitant response of "quality," which suggested something about the distractions in the company and possibly the lack of *focus.*

In the two years leading up to my year as President of the National Restaurant Association (NRA), I asked fellow board members and the staff, "What is our biggest weakness as an industry?" The NRA had been in existence for 74 years and was a very reputable organization, but it had a history of being reactive to legislative and regulatory issues. This situation was due in part to the apathy of an industry that has enjoyed many years of growth and success, a lack of unity on core issues confronting the industry, and quite frankly, the fact that people were more concerned about their own lives and businesses until there was an immediate threat. But the magnitude of the legislative threat to our industry and free enterprise was becoming so burdensome that we had to become more proactive and more united in our positions. This had been the sentiment of many of our members and the staff, so it occurred to me that an appropriate theme during my year as president might be…"One Voice."

More often than not, asking the right questions avoids developing a new "mouse trap" when all we needed to do was better utilize the one we had. Asking the right questions produces more of the right decisions. It is possible, however, to make the "right" decisions and still not achieve the desired result. That's poor execution and weak management of the details. In that case, you have another question to ask…do I have the right people?

Get Ugly

Sometimes it is necessary to raise the sense of urgency of a key decision to another level in order to initiate the proper action with the appropriate level of urgency. I call this the "get ugly" principle. Use it sparingly or people will begin to question your emotional stability.

During my first 60 days at Godfather's Pizza I asked the Director of Human Resources (HR) when we had last conducted HR audits in our restaurants. An HR audit simply verifies that all legally required notices are properly posted and that documentation on each restaurant employee is available and current. If they are not, we would be subject to fines by the Department of Labor—the last thing on which I wanted to spend money.

The HR director informed me that we had never done HR audits. This happened during a staff meeting with my direct reports, causing me to have a conniption fit (some called it a "**Cain**niption"). I directed the HR chief to immediately perform an HR audit on all 200 company restaurants. I also asked him to not let me see him in Omaha (not even on weekends) until he had finished that task. I excused him from the meeting so he could begin right away. He completed the task in an amazingly short period of time, after which he returned to staff meetings and his other HR duties.

The right question in this instance was, "When was the last time we performed HR audits in our company restaurants?" The wrong answer was, "What's an HR audit?"

Asking the right questions can take many forms, from the type of questions in the previous examples to requesting the preparation of a formal presentation of strategic and operating plans on a periodic basis. In either case, if the questions are not asked then problems can go undetected.

Along the way, developing and selecting the right alternative to a problem or opportunity can range from a "no brainer" to a very complicated analysis. But the person or persons closest to the situation can usually provide the best starting set of alternatives from which to choose. These alternatives also provide the basis for additional alternatives that so often emerge from the creative processes of discussion, review, and listening.

Even the best laid plans can run into problems. When this happens, the leader must keep things on track and on time by effectively dealing with obstacles, or making sure someone has the delegated authority to do so.

Leaders must look, listen, learn, and then lead.

INSPIRE

The American Heritage Dictionary defines *inspire* as "to stimulate to creativity or action." My own variation on this definition is "to stimulate positive action," which means to add to what is already there. A person's determination can be inspired to a higher level. Their belief in something can be inspired, their inner energy can be inspired, their faith can be inspired, their motivation can be inspired to a higher level, and so forth. Inspiration is motivation plus emotion.

A leader's ability to inspire is determined most by the ability to communicate with words and symbolic actions. Words, phrases, and sentences delivered convincingly or with convincing passion inspire people. Passion is not always necessary to inspire using words, but believability is a requirement. The same words delivered by different individuals can have a totally different impact on another person or group of people, just as two different actors in a play or movie can cause the audience to have two different emotional experiences. Most of us have experienced someone trying to tell a funny story when it was just not that funny…something was missing in the delivery.

A leader's credibility while attempting to inspire the troops is most often enhanced by the leader's past accomplishments, his or her formal credentials, a shared belief or point of view, personal characteristics such as reputation for high integrity, D-E-F leadership characteristics, or charisma (personal magnetism or charm).

When I came to Godfather's Pizza and boldly stated in my opening speech that GPI could succeed, it was believable because I had taken a poorly performing Burger King region and turned it around (which was one of the reasons I was selected to become President of Godfather's Pizza). In fact, my entire career had been deemed a "meteoric" rise in the corporate world. So why not believe this guy when he said the company could win again?

Obviously, not everyone is born a gifted orator, but most leaders can become at least good speakers if they work at it. The leader who "pooh-poohs" the value of being able to inspire his people through the spoken word will miss many opportunities to enhance performance, productivity, and creativity.

Most people like to win, to be on a winning team, or to be a part of a winning effort. The desire to win inspires people, and a leader who projects a winning attitude or winning ways attracts people who want to win. No one that I know wakes up in the morning hoping their day will be a failure.

If done appropriately, symbolic actions can inspire as well as words. The most obvious symbolic action that can inspire occurs when the leader accomplishes what he or she says they are going to achieve or when the leader reaches a predetermined benchmark. In some instances, it is inspiring when the leader just "rolls up his sleeves" with the workers.

When I had the "Cainniption" fit about the lack of HR audits, it sent a message about the importance of being in compliance with appropriate legal requirements. The "fit" inspired other departments to assess their compliance activities to avoid a "Cainniption." Now, I am not suggesting that this will work for everyone—of course it will not. It worked for me because of my personality and my personal leadership style. I tried to do it in such a way that while the message was serious, the HR director understood that the problem was the target of the "Cainniption," not the person.

An unexpected bonus, or salary increase, or an unexpected day off for a job exceptionally well done, or remembering a new employee's name are all symbolic actions which are capable of inspiring. A leader must be able to inspire people to achieve more than they would if he/she were not the leader.

After my town hall meeting "chat" with President Clinton, many people wrote to me or called expressing how happy they were to see me asking the President the "right question" and informing him of the errors in his calculations. Many people went on to comment that they were now inspired to write or call their own senators or congressional representatives because they shared my views about the negative impact of his health care plan on jobs. I never expected one event to inspire so many people to speak up and to speak out. The restaurant industry became especially mobilized against the plan because of the disproportionately large number of entry level and first-time workers our industry hires and the relatively high employee turnover rate.

That first GPI system-wide speech I gave in 1986 (see Chapter 2) inspired people to believe more than they already did about Godfather's Pizza's opportunity to be successful again. Although many of the people who heard that speech shared my belief about our potential for success, even more of the audience was inspired because they were convinced that I believed what I was saying...and I did. As we began to successfully implement some of the ideas we had developed as a management team and to achieve some of our goals, the credibility of that opening speech was enhanced.

We also deliberately redefined some measures of success so people in the company would know if we were winning or not—because winning inspires. How much fun would it be to go bowling where there's a sheet in front of the pins so you could not see them fall? You could hear them but you would not know how you were scoring. Pretty soon you would become uninspired to continue.

For the first two decades of Godfather's Pizza's existence, the primary measure of success was how many restaurants we built as a system and how fast we built them. This was no longer appropriate since the pizza segment, and the restaurant industry as a whole, were showing slower growth. So we refocused on growth in per unit volume as a primary measure of success. We were also not looking for the "home run" idea because successive "hits" would still allow us to score—and we did.

One year after I became President of Godfather's Pizza we had 200 fewer units, but per unit sales were showing positive increases month after month. We were winning again—and the people were excited!

Words or actions or achievements which *inspire* people can range from subtle to blatant, but what works for one leader versus another is a function of individual personality and style. Tangible results will always inspire but when results are sometimes slow to materialize, the critical ability to inspire in creative ways is what distinguishes "leadership" from "positionship."

CHAPTER 2

MOVING UP
THE LADDER

THINKING

If you think you are beaten, you are.
If you think you dare not, you don't.
If you'd like to win but you think you can't,
It's almost a cinch you won't.

If you think you'll lose, you're lost,
For out of the world we find
Success begins with a fellow's will—
It's all in the state of mind.

If you think you're outclassed, you are;
You've got to think high to rise;
You've got to be sure of yourself before
You can ever win a prize.

Life's battle doesn't always go
To stronger or faster men;
But sooner or later the man who wins,
Is the one who thinks he can.

Walter D. Wintle

The Pillsbury Company Experience

LOOKING FOR PROBLEMS

In 1976 The Pillsbury Company (TPC) was 107 years old, with approximately 1.5 billion dollars in sales. An article on the front page of the Wall Street Journal featured Pillsbury's Chairman and CEO, Bill Spoor, who was quoted as saying that in five years TPC would be a five billion dollar company. This seemed extremely aggressive since it had taken 107 years to reach 1.5 billion dollars. While reading that article it occurred to me that such a growth rate would create some growing pains and some problems and opportunities that required a good corporate problem solver. And, there just might be a vice president position in one of those opportunities along the way. This was just wishful thinking on my part, since I had started to feel that my opportunities to move up at the Coca Cola Company were limited (D-factor).

I was working at the Coca-Cola Company as a corporate manager of management science, applying my mathematics and computer science background but not managing anyone except myself. The title "manager" was in my job description just in case I needed to "manage" someone on a special project, and to justify my salary to the personnel department (it wasn't called human resources yet). What the job really consisted of was business analysis and problem solving.

A few weeks after the Wall Street Journal article appeared, Bob Copper (my boss) announced to his group of four managers of management science that he had accepted a new job at The Pillsbury Company in Minneapolis. What a coincidence, I thought to myself, because we had no idea that Pillsbury was recruiting him to establish a corporate business analysis and problem-solving function similar to the one he had created so successfully at the Coca-Cola Company.

A few months later I saw Bob at a conference in Miami, where we had a chance to visit and get caught up on how things were going. I had worked for Bob at the Coca-Cola Company for nearly four years and we had also become friends. When I asked about his new job he said he liked it, but he badly needed to upgrade the staff he had inherited. Most of his people were technically competent but lacked the communications skills necessary to effectively "merchandize" the analytical results to the business units.

He then talked about Pillsbury's aggressive growth plans and the kinds of problems his business analysis function faced...economic analysis, business portfolio analysis, manufacturing plant site selection, acquisitions analysis, marketing analysis, systems analysis, and the list went on. Even more, Bob indicated that the CEO was dead serious about becoming a 5 billion dollar company in five years. After talking for a while it began to sound as though my earlier speculation about the need for a good problem solver was, in fact, a need for a few good problem solvers.

Bob then started to casually discuss the possibility of me coming to work for him at TPC. My first thought was, "In that weather?!" I had been to Minneapolis on a job interview when I was nearing graduation from college. It was in February of all months. I had never been that cold or seen that much snow in my life, not even on TV. The thought of living in Minneapolis was a new paradigm for me, not to mention trying to convince my wife, Gloria, to move. Think about it...I was working for a good company with a "good job" that I could probably maintain for the next 35 years, and then retire comfortably...living in our home town of Atlanta where the weather was moderate and not extreme. Why would anyone in their right mind give that up?

Within a couple of months of that meeting, Bob made me an offer to join him at Pillsbury. He told me quite frankly that the job was a risky venture because his challenge was to bring more structured analysis to the decision-making process at Pillsbury, especially given its aggressive growth objectives. He felt that I could help him achieve that goal. If we succeeded, then other career opportunities might be available. If we did not succeed, "Well," he said, "we could both be looking for new jobs." The possibility of success excited me more than the possibility of failure, so I accepted his offer to join The Pillsbury Company (E-factor).

YOUNG WHIPPER-SNAPPER

The challenge and risks were certainly clear, the compensation significantly more, and the opportunity as manager of business analysis with six people to manage (for real this time) was exciting. The weather was never an issue, but I knew Bob well enough to complain about it to get him to sweeten the offer. To my surprise, the weather really was not a big issue with Gloria as long as she and our five-year-old daughter, Melanie, could keep warm in the winter and cool in the summer.

Things went well. In less than two years, the business analysis department was making a difference and its credibility was well established. I was even promoted to Director of the 16-person department after Bob was promoted to a new job. Twelve months after that, I was promoted again to Director of the consumer products division's information systems function, consisting of over 100 people. The consumer products division was the largest division of the company, with a lot of acquisitions activity. In my new job, I reported to the Vice President of Corporate Systems; Bob had meanwhile become Vice President of Strategic Planning. As our career paths began to go in separate but equally successful directions, opportunities opened up because new jobs were finding us.

About a year later, Pillsbury acquired the Green Giant Company, nearly the size of the consumer products division. This meant consolidating the two respective large systems functions now totaling over 200 people. I was selected to head the combined organization, which was another promotion and the most challenging leadership responsibility of my career. The continuity of the business computer applications had to be maintained; some positions had to be eliminated because of duplicate responsibilities, naturally causing anxiety within the organization; the two totally different organizational cultures now had to become one; and the systems architecture of the two companies was totally opposite (one centralized, the other modular). I was also younger than all of the senior-level people in both systems functions, causing some of them to wonder if this young "whipper-snapper" at 33 years of age could lead.

The consolidation of the two systems functions went smoothly after a lot of planning and, most importantly, a lot of communicating to everyone involved (*removing* communications as a *barrier*). First, I communicated with everyone honestly and openly. Second, I talked with the business units about their needs and expectations. Third, I asked the senior-level people to design the consolidated organizational structure without specifying who would head the various departments. Fourth, I became familiar with all the senior-level people from the Green Giant systems function, both formally and informally, before I decided who would fill the "boxes" on the organizational chart. Fifth, those people that did not have the opportunity to stay received very generous severance packages. Sixth, I did not hesitate to seek the advice and counsel of my new boss, the Corporate Vice President of Systems, Dr. John Haaland. The transition over the subsequent twelve months exceeded our expectations. The planning and communications had paid off, though we were always mindful that Murphy's Law could materialize at any time…but it didn't!

A year after the Green Giant acquisition, TPC achieved another record increase in sales and earnings per share growth. The two computer systems and the culture of the two organizations had been successfully blended into a positive and proactive function.

We had established a more personable working relationship with our customers, who were the people in the business units and other staff functions needing computer systems and programming expertise. I insisted that we approach our customers to help them determine their requirements, rather than the traditional practice of sitting by the phone and waiting until they called with a request. This also helped to debunk the growing myth that computer people were "smart but weird." We wanted to help solve the business problems and not just the computer problems *(lead)*.

When I initially visited with the business executives after being named director of the combined function, they indicated that being on time and on budget was one of the biggest frustrations in the systems department. We made project deadlines more realistic, and stuck to our commitments even if people had to work a little longer or a little faster. We were now able to minimize our customers' frustrations.

In addition to meeting regularly with my department heads, I met periodically with everyone in the department so that they would have an appreciation of activities and projects outside of their respective departments, as well as a greater appreciation of how their jobs were important to the overall objectives of the entire systems organizations. To further enhance communications, we held a summer picnic and a Christmas party, where people in the organization discovered that many of their colleagues had "smarts" *and* personalities.

Although direct feedback from customers, regular and periodic communications with everyone in the organization, and informal activities may seem simple and common sense, they are often overshadowed by the demands of the technical and business-related "stuff" that take most of the leader's attention. But a little attention to the people goes a long way toward achieving a lot of results *(inspire)*.

Our customers were happier, my people were happier, and my boss was happy *(achieve desired results)*. Everything was running smoothly as I was beginning to become seasoned in this large leadership responsibility. A learning curve can be accelerated, but experience takes time, and I was beginning to gain some serious seasoning in my position as Director of Information Systems.

DID YOU SAY VICE PRESIDENT?

I was attending a summer workshop of the Institute of Management Science on a small college campus in New York State when I received a message to call my boss, Dr. John Haaland. It was unusual for John to track me down like that, so naturally I wondered if we had a systems crisis. I had just arrived that afternoon, and the attendees were having dinner when I went to a pay phone to call John.

He asked me if I could be back in Minneapolis the next morning. Bill Spoor, the CEO, wanted to make an announcement. I said, "He doesn't need my permission…what's the big deal, I'm not even near a major airport." The big deal was that John had decided to leave Pillsbury to pursue something he had always wanted to do, and Bill Spoor wanted to make the announcement that I was to be John's replacement. I knew I was one of the people John had identified as a possible successor, but I didn't know he was serious about this. Bill Spoor wanted to make the announcement in the morning and wanted me to be there to be introduced as the new Vice President of Corporate Systems *and* Services.

"Did you say vice president?" I asked. John said, "Yes. Congratulations!" When I asked how to get there by the next morning, he told me that a Pillsbury corporate jet was on its way to the local airport to pick me up, and that it would take me back after the announcement. Wow, was I excited!

I called Gloria and gave her the news before going back to the dinner. I announced to the attendees that I had suddenly lost my appetite, and that I would be leaving but returning tomorrow afternoon. I told them of my appointment to vice president and the Chairman's announcement the next morning. The group was excited for me and applauded the announcement.

W hen I took over as the Vice President of Corporate Systems and Services, I was responsible for the computer operations function which processed all business applications for all of Pillsbury's Minneapolis-based businesses. I also oversaw the long-range strategic systems planning for the company, corporate systems programming and development, and three major new initiatives that were underway. Fortunately, I inherited a very competent staff from John and did not have to replace any senior-level people. This allowed me to *focus* on completion of the three new initiatives.

The first initiative was a new mainframe computer for the Minneapolis-based businesses. This project was proceeding well technically, but I would have to make my first presentation to the Pillsbury Board of Directors to get approval for the capital expenditure. Concurrent with this initiative was the construction of a new offsite state-of-the-art data processing facility to house the new hardware. I obtained approval for these two initiatives, and they proceeded as planned.

WORLD HEADQUARTERS PROJECT

The third initiative was the Pillsbury World Headquarters Project (WHP). A new twin-tower, 40-floor office complex was being constructed by a real estate developer in downtown Minneapolis, and Pillsbury was to be the major tenant occupying the majority of the office space. At that time the company had people working in nine different locations throughout the greater Minneapolis area, with people as far away as LeSueur, Minnesota, where Green Giant had been headquartered for years. In addition to space requirements for the executive officers and the various corporate functions, space was also required for the consumer products division, the agricultural products division, the restaurant division, the international division, and several smaller business units. This required space for nearly 2,000 people.

The World Headquarters Project was over budget, behind schedule, and headed for a "crash" with our future landlord. Although the landlord had control of the construction project with its own set of requirements and specifications, Pillsbury had certain agreed-upon rights and privileges for its space requirements as the major tenant. The problem was that sometimes these requirements were in conflict due to language ambiguities in the lease document. These ambiguities caused conflicts over who would pay for changes in the project. We were not talking peanuts, we were talking millions of dollars in real money. This "debate" caused the landlord to have a full-time staff of lawyers assigned to work on it, and I also had a full-time staff of lawyers (which I had inherited) to work with me on Pillsbury's behalf.

The WHP was not part of John Haaland's area of responsibility prior to his departure; it was being run by another executive who was nearing retirement and who was not experienced in leading large systems projects. Nor was I, for that matter, experienced on projects as broad as this one, but once again I would rely on my *common sense* instincts to get me through...I hoped! By *asking the right questions,* it became clear that the WHP had little to do with bricks and mortar, and more to do with a massive systems problem. Thus, John had suggested that it be part of my new job since the systems consolidation and transition of the Green Giant and Consumer Division a year earlier had gone so well.

The previous executive had briefed me on the project, so I decided to call a meeting of all the players on the Pillsbury project team to introduce myself and to get their perspectives. I had asked my predecessor to only invite the key person from each major area to this first meeting.

When I walked into the meeting room there were 20 people in attendance not counting my predecessor, my secretary, and myself. I was shocked because I expected about 10 or 12. After I introduced myself and told them how I planned to get up to speed, I asked for questions or comments. They nodded politely but no one asked any questions. I later discovered during one-on-one meetings with each of these 20 key people that they all had an uneasy sense about this project *ever* getting done, and quite frankly, they wanted to know what this young "whipper-snapper" was supposed to "bring to the party" and the current state of confusion.

When I asked what the project needed most, they said someone who can and will make some decisions so we can get on with the project. As I was told, too many decisions had to get Bill Spoor's direct approval. This often created delays, which is understandable since his main *focus* was trying to achieve another record year of sales earnings growth. The delays compounded the issues we were trying to resolve with our future landlord.

All of the people on the project appeared very competent and had been mutually complimentary during the one-on-one discussions. My focus was now very clear...remove the communications barriers and get this project moving!

I started by having an extended discussion with Bill Spoor, the CEO, about what he wanted to see and what he did not want to see as part of the new World Headquarters facility. I had this same discussion with the President and COO of the company, Win Wallin. They were both clear about their expectations. These expectations became my "marching orders," since they were the two main customers. When I met with business unit heads, I asked them what they wanted to see within the framework of my direction from Mr. Spoor and Mr. Wallin.

I did not go back and ask Bill or Win for another decision after that, although I did provide them with periodic updates on the status of the project. During these updates with both Spoor and Wallin in the room at the same time, not once did they tell me I did not have the authority to make some of the decisions I had obviously made concerning the project. This was my first experience with the old saying "it is better to ask forgiveness than to ask permission" (but be prepared to take your beating if you are wrong).

I had decided in my own mind, however, that I would ask their approval only if it involved spending more money than had already been approved in the total budget, or if a decision could potentially expand our legal liability in some way. In neither instance did that occur.

The next major barrier was our relationship with our future land-lord and some unresolved issues, such as the size of the letters in the atrium of the building identifying the Pillsbury tower versus the size of the letters identifying the next largest tenant in the building in the adjacent tower. The more substantive issues related to the cost of numerous changes that had been requested and who would pay. I found myself in countless meetings with my counterpart, his lawyers and staff, and my lawyers and staff. We spent more time trying to fig-ure out who should attend the meetings to avoid having 40 people at every meeting than we did resolving the issues.

After weeks of this frustrating and unproductive exercise, I finally said to my counterpart, "Let's have a meeting without the lawyers and without any of our staff people who are working on the project...just you and me." He agreed it was a good idea. My attorney objected to such a meeting because he thought "they" might try to pull a fast one on me because I was new to the project. Since I *was* in charge I thanked my attorney for his input and then proceeded to plan a date for an extensive one-on-one meeting *(lead)*.

When we met, we found that we agreed on more things than we disagreed on, and we were able to reach resolutions on a lot of things without "my lawyer" talking to "his lawyer." We discussed what direc-tion we would give our staffs on the remaining unresolved issues and identified ways for reaching resolution even if we did not currently agree. We both had to make some compromises, but we found it a lot easier to do with two people in the room rather than 40 *(remove barriers)*.

The project started to pick up momentum! All decisions got made without having to ask permission, and all issues were resolved with our landlord to avoid a "crash" except for one remaining issue...the size of the letters in the atrium for the respective towers. My coun-terpart and I agreed to a resolution that would not make either of our bosses happy, so we decided not to put them in the position to say "no." We ordered the letters and had them constructed just prior to move in *(E-factor)*. When the project was completed *below budget* and *ahead of* its original schedule, no one asked about the size of the letters.

Two years after the World Headquarters Project was completed, I was presented a Symbol of Excellence in Leadership Award by The Pillsbury Company. Mr. Spoor made the presentation.

I'M BORED

Well, the new data center was completed, the new computer system was installed and working, and the World Headquarters Project was done and everyone had moved into their new offices. My job at this point consisted mostly of maintaining what we had accomplished.

One day while sitting in my new office on the 31st floor of the new headquarters building, I looked out of my window and saw that the inflatable dome of the new Minneapolis stadium had collapsed. It was during this time that I started to feel as if my motivation had also collapsed, even though life was good. My wife and I were healthy, and we now had a daughter and a son. We had a nice home that we had finished decorating, and all our bills were up to date. We even started taking real vacations, which we had never done much earlier in my career. I was even singing in the church choir again, and recording with a Minneapolis gospel singing group. Life was real good but something was missing from my job. Then one day it hit me…I'm bored.

I realized that the excitement, challenge, and risk of the last few years had kept me happy and motivated. My father's health was not good due to complications with diabetes. He had always been one of my heroes. I thought about how much he had been able to accomplish in his life with a lot less than I had started with, and how much difference he had made to so many people and especially to me.

As I contemplated these things at the "old" age of 36, and having been blessed to achieve so much so fast, I knew I had to reach for more. I had so enjoyed my exposure to the leaders of the business units that I started to imagine how exciting it might be to actually be the decision maker running a business. All of my career I had recommended what the business decision maker should do, or managed a "cost center," but I started some wishful thinking again…"Maybe I could become a President of something, somewhere, for somebody, someday." Hmmm *(D-factor)!*

I really did not know how to get there but I knew within Pillsbury that a vice president of systems would not be handed a business to run. One day it was announced that the President of Pillsbury's Poppin Fresh Restaurants had resigned. I made an appointment with Win Wallin, President of Pillsbury, and went in and asked him for that job. He seemed stunned, and asked me why I wanted it. I explained to him that I was not really expecting him to say "yes," but that I did have a desire to run a business someday. He suggested that I would need to learn a business from the ground up before I could run one effectively. He said I also needed to gain some experience with profit and loss responsibility and build some credibility for running a business, which would help me down the road in trying to lead a company.

When I asked if he had any other ideas of where I could learn a business, he suggested Burger King or one of Pillsbury's other restaurant concepts, because they made up half of Pillsbury's portfolio and they were growing and needed all the management talent they could find. He said he would call the presidents of Burger King and Steak & Ale and ask them to talk to me if I were interested, and then told me to take it from there.

I called Hal Smith, President of the Steak & Ale and Bennigan's chains, and set up a time when I could visit him. I had met Hal at a Pillsbury Board of Directors dinner, where he had just been appointed to his position about the same time I was appointed to Vice President of Systems and Services. That had been two years earlier, and we had not visited since. I flew to his office in Dallas where we had a very nice meeting, but I sensed that even though Win had talked to him, he really did not know what to tell me or what to do with me. He wished me luck, and I moved on.

When I visited with Lou Neeb, the President of Burger King, he was more definitive. He said Win had highly recommended me and that BKC had a "fast-track" program to the vice president and regional manager (RVP) level. It was for people with management and leadership skills that wanted to get into operations. BKC had ten operating regions headed by an RVP, one of the most coveted positions in the company.

Lou went on to explain that the program would take about a year and a half and it would start me in a restaurant "at the bottom," which would allow me to really learn the business. He said that he could not guarantee that I would make it to the vice president and regional manager level, nor could he commit to where I would be assigned *if* I made it through the program. He said, "But at least you can do your training in Minneapolis so you will not have to move yet."…Whoopie! When I asked about compensation he said, "Oh yes, you would also have to take a cut in compensation until you finished the program." I said, "What happens if I do not make it through the program?" His response was, "I guess you will probably be looking for another job." Seems like I had heard that before.

A couple of weeks later I received a description of the "fast track" program in writing, with an offer to join BKC as described above. I had had plenty of time to discuss it with Gloria, who was extremely supportive of my decision. I assured her that we would not "starve" if this did not work out, because I am never too proud to work any job that I have to in order to take care of my family. But if this did work out, who knew where it could lead. Once again, the possibility of success excited me more than the possibility of failure. I accepted their offer to go into the "fast track" program…with no guarantees *(E-factor)*.

My start date was April of 1982, which was also the month that Jeff Campbell had been appointed the new President of Burger King.

Jeff had been through the "fast track" program himself. I was encouraged to hear this until I learned that he was one of the few people to ever complete the program. Before that, he had been the Executive Vice President of Marketing for Burger King Corporation. At this point I had already resigned from Pillsbury.

The people I had worked with at Pillsbury gave me a farewell reception to wish me well on my career change and to recognize me for my contributions while at TPC. On the day of the reception, which was held in a large activities room near my office on the 31st floor of the World Headquarters building, my secretary pulled me out of the reception where there were hundreds of well-wishers. She said my brother was on the phone; I went into my office and took the call.

My father had died. We had been expecting this because of Dad's illness, but now the finality of it was real. I sat and prayed for a while in quiet and gathered my emotions. I knew we needed to make arrangements to go to Atlanta, but I tried to imagine what Dad would have wanted me to do about that reception. He would have wanted me to go back in and finish it, which I did. I even gave "thank you" remarks at the end. Gloria was attending the reception but I did not tell her about Dad until it was over. She was also very fond of my father.

When I left Pillsbury I never looked back. I knew that the coincidence of Dad's passing was a message that I had to succeed.

I was motivated again.

Slippery Tracks at Burger King Corporation

WELCOME TO BURGER KING

I reported to the Bloomington training restaurant in the Minneapolis region, where I was issued a crew uniform, a set of operations manuals, a training manual, and my schedule for the week. I started my "fast-track" training at the back of the broiler. The broiler person is responsible for putting buns and patties through the broiler. This was the first position I learned as I eventually progressed through all the positions in the restaurant. Assignment to the next position was based on developing some proficiency at each previous position. Before the end of the day, I was assigned to the front of the broiler to learn the steamer position. I was off and running.

After a few weeks of learning the broiler, steamer, burger board, whopper board, specialty sandwich board, and fry station in the "back of the house," I then worked the positions of cashier, expediter, drive-thru order taker, runner-bagger, and drink station in the "front of the house." Not long afterwards, I attended a week of classroom operations training at the regional training center for assistant managers. After more in-restaurant practice came another week of classroom training before attending Burger King University (BKU) in Miami, BKC's headquarters.

By early summer I had successfully completed my in-restaurant and classroom basic training. I was then assigned to the Hopkins, Minnesota unit as the fourth assistant manager. This restaurant was an average-volume Burger King restaurant, which sometimes required two managers during busy periods. I was no longer the "young whipper-snapper," I was that "old dude" (36) from Pillsbury. In addition, I could sense that the managers and assistants were wondering why they were "fast tracking" this guy through to become an RVP.

Soon I was being scheduled to run the busy shifts, lunch or dinner, as the solo assistant manager on duty. This went smoothly as long as everyone scheduled to work showed up, they were well-trained at their positions, and nothing unusual went wrong. Unlike the consolidation of the Pillsbury Consumer Products and Green Giant systems functions, "Murphy's Law" appeared on a regular basis.

NO BURGERS

I had a young Asian man, Quan, working the steamer position. He spoke very little English but he was dependable and hard-working, and once he learned how to do a position he would do it with tenacity and strictly by the book. One day during a busy lunch period, his foot accidentally got tangled in the flexible gas hose connected to the broiler and inadvertently cut the gas off to the broiler. It was so busy that no one noticed this had happened until Mary Pat, who was working the burger board, called me from the front of the restaurant and said the patties were undercooked. Thinking I needed to adjust the broiler temperature, I went to do so and noticed dozens of burger patties coming out of the front of the broiler not cooked at all. Quan had been taught to put the patties in the buns and then put them in the steamer where they were held until the burgers and whoppers were to be finished. He was working so fast that he did not notice the meat was not being cooked properly.

Fortunately, Mary Pat had informed me in time and none of the raw patties made it out of the steamer. The broiler had gradually cooled down after the gas was accidentally shut off, causing gradual undercooking of both burger patties and whopper patties. The broiler would take at least 15 minutes to get back up to cooking temperature.

The lines at the counter were backed up to the front door, cars in the drive-thru lane were wrapped all the way around the restaurant and into the street, and we had no burgers at Burger King! In class they never taught me what to do in this situation...common sense leadership, where are you?

I asked Mary Pat to restart the broiler and told the person on specialty sandwiches (chicken and fish) to make as many as they could as fast as the operations manual would allow. I told the drink person to just start pouring soft drinks in all sizes and all flavors as fast as the machine would go. "Drop fries" was the phrase we used to let the fry station person know that we needed more fries cooked. I told him to, "Keep dropping fries until I tell you to stop" *(leaders must lead)*.

I then went into the front of the restaurant and got the attention of the customers and told them that our broiler had malfunctioned and it would be 15 minutes before we could serve burgers or whoppers again. I apologized for the inconvenience and informed them that we had plenty of chicken, fish, fries, soft drinks, and milk shakes. I recall only a handful of people leaving the crowded foyer of the restaurant. Similarly, I walked outside and went from car to car in the drive-thru lane explaining the situation until I had talked to each and every customer *(E-factor)*. Again, only a few decided to leave.

By the time the broiler was working again and we were back in the burger business, we were completely sold out of chicken and fish sandwiches, but customers were happy. Quan had learned a valuable lesson, and I had made it through my first "fast track" crisis and the first appearance of "Murphy."

MYSTERY OF THE $50

One night I was working the evening shift, which meant I had to close down the restaurant. This involved taking the daily inventory, cleaning and sanitizing equipment, cleaning the restaurant in preparation for the next day, and counting and balancing the cash receipts with the recorded register receipts. The restaurant closed at 11 p.m., and it usually took a couple of hours maximum to finish all the closing duties. That night my cash count came up $50 short of my register receipts. Restaurant procedures required that you be "written up" in your personnel file if you were more than $25 short without a good explanation. I recounted every cashier's drawer over and over trying to find the discrepancy, since I did not want the "old dude" to be "written up." I could have taken $50 of my own money and put it in the cash to avoid the embarrassment, but I decided to do it by the book. Finally, at 5 a.m. I recorded the $50 shortage on the reconciliation form and went home, puzzled. I had to be back at work at 2 p.m. for my next night shift.

The next night I closed the restaurant again, and my cash reconciliation came up $50 over! I recounted again and again, but could not find the discrepancy. So for the week my nightly cash report balanced out as it should. It would be months before I would find out what happened to the mysterious $50.

I was rapidly gaining the respect of the other managers and the crew because they realized that I was not looking for any special treatment. I was working night shift, day shift, weekends, substitute shifts, and sometimes a shift and a half or whenever I was scheduled. Not only could I do all the functions in the restaurant, but I *would* do any of them, especially if we had a lot of no-shows.

In addition to the "no burgers" and "the mysterious $50" incidents, I experienced a lot in four months. I lived through Friday night disturbances in the parking lot which sometimes required the police, and product inventory delivery right in the middle of a lunch rush. I was working one Saturday when the RVP stopped in with his family for lunch and did not like the way his whopper was made (by the book); I was then treated to the district manager screaming at me on Monday about the incident in the kitchen while other crew members observed him chewing me out. I would often lend a listening ear to teenagers with school and family problems, or offer encouragement to people just trying to "make it." These experiences taught me nothing about how to manage the restaurant profit-and-loss statements, but they taught me a lot about how to manage the business.

HAPPY B.E.E.s

After two months of basic training and two months as an assistant manager at the Hopkins, Minnesota Burger King, I was assigned manager of the restaurant in August of 1982. Now I was really responsible for everything, including the scheduling of the assistants and crew, reordering of product inventory, cash procedures, security, hiring and firing of crew members, and the P&L (profit and loss) for the restaurant.

My district manager challenged me to find ways to keep the restaurant on sales projection and, if possible, improve the current sales trend of $850,000 for the year. As restaurant manager, I was not at liberty to change prices, marketing, promotions, or the menu, and there was a whole list of other "don'ts," but I was supposed to increase the sales in the restaurant. The only thing he didn't tell me not to change was the attitude of everybody working in the restaurant *(E-factor)*.

Ah ha! I thought to myself, what if I could come up with a way to make it more fun for the largely teenage crew working in the unit. This might cause them to be genuinely nicer to customers, which might make them come back more often. But I knew it would require more than just a speech about "let's smile more."

While traveling back from an operations training class at Burger King University, I got the idea of an awareness tool that would remind everyone in the restaurant to focus more on service, with a noticeably higher level of friendliness.

Instead of referring to everyone as crew members, I called them "happy B.E.E.s" after each member consistently demonstrated the "happy B.E.E." attitude . . .

B - Bad moods stay at home

E - Eye contact with the customer

E - Every day!

Although I realize that not everyone is an overly expressive social butterfly, and that there are days when everyone (including me) has a "bad mood" day, we simply had to leave the bad moods at home, because bad moods, just like good moods, are contagious. It was the power of positive thinking.

I also realized that not everyone is an unaided "smiler," but I had learned that if you look someone in the eye and smile, then *most* people return the smile. If you do not believe this, try it sometime, but don't try it on a street corner at night wearing a trench coat or you could get arrested. Try it at home, at work, on an airplane with the person sitting next to you, or when you pass someone in a hallway, and if you look sincere about it, they will respond.

So I challenged all members of the crew to learn how to look the customers in the eye when greeting them, taking their orders, or saying "thank you." This was easier for some than others, but shortly we had enough happy B.E.E.s every day so that I could assign only happy B.E.E.s to work the front counter serving the customers.

Naturally, there were skeptics and some of the teenagers thought it was corny at first. But soon, they started to enjoy it because they realized it was much nicer serving happy customers who smiled back. Also, it made work more fun. The attitude at the front counter was also contagious to those working in the "back of the house," where I also insisted that "bad moods stay at home"...every day.

The key that made it work was being a serious happy B.E.E. myself. We reinforced the practice with T-shirts, caps, buttons, and even "happy B.E.E. bucks," redeemable for gifts. I also made sure to inform the team of our sales trend, which started to increase about two months after the start of the happy B.E.E. program.

When I first started the happy B.E.E. program, a young lady named Denise worked the front counter. She was very pleasant and dependable but she never seemed to be very happy and she hardly ever smiled. I told her several times that she had to try making eye contact or I would have to reassign her to a work station in the kitchen, which she did not like. She did not believe me, so I did. After working the broiler for about two days, Denise came to me and said she was ready to try being a "happy B.E.E." I gave her the chance and she did great! I detected later that her original reluctance was caused by shyness, which had temporarily been a barrier to her own motivation. Once she started to look people in the eye consciously, her self-confidence improved. Obviously, I was proud of her and she became one of my best "happy B.E.E.s."

One day near the end of a lunch shift I was checking the dining room of the restaurant when a customer stopped me and asked if I was the manager. I said "Yes. What's wrong?," since you don't usually expect customers to stop you to say something is good. The lady was sitting at a table where she could see the entire front counter area and she had already finished her lunch. She asked, "How do you get so many happy people at the front counter?" I smiled (relieved) and said, "Thank you," but thought to myself, "Yes!" The lady went on to tell me that she had noticed this consistency over the past several weeks and that she actually had started to come in more often…"ching, ching ($)" *(achieved desired results)*.

The idea of giving "exceptional service" was not new to Burger King when I arrived, but the barrier was how to inspire an entire group or a shy Denise to be self-motivated to do so. Instead of just saying "smile," I gave them a technique to help them smile, which in turn made the customers happier. Instead of just saying "have fun while we work," we made work fun. Instead of expecting new sales to fall from the sky, we gave our existing customers a compelling reason to come back more often, and they did!

Three months into being manager of the Hopkins BK restaurant and about two months into the Happy B.E.E. program, our sales trend was up over projection by more than 20 percent. This caused my district manager, Dave, to revise the projection for the year from $850,000 to $1,000,000. In fact, he implemented the happy B.E.E. program in all of the restaurants in his seven-store district. Before I knew it, I was giving a happy B.E.E. presentation at his district meeting for managers. As you would expect, the managers that embraced the concept achieved more impact on their sales, and soon Dave's district was showing the greatest year over year comparable sales increases in the region. *It all started by focusing on what I could do rather than on what I was told not to do.*

With the restaurant and the district doing noticeably better than expected, the RVP told his boss in Miami that he thought I was ready for a regional vice president assignment. I did not know this until later, but I knew something was up when I was assigned to "shadow" a franchise district manager and an area manager for a month each.

In December, I got a call to fly to BK headquarters in Miami to meet with the Division Vice President of the five eastern regions. I was told that I was being promoted to RVP for the Philadelphia region, which covered seven adjacent states and the District of Columbia. I was both excited and surprised because I had been in the fast-track program only nine months instead of the 18-month original plan. I guess they underestimated the "old dude" from Pillsbury (age *barrier removed*).

The assistant managers that worked for me were also excited for me when they heard the news, because by now we had developed a high level of mutual respect for each other. My district manager, Dave, was also happy for me but hated to lose the inventor of the happy B.E.E. program.

One of the assistant managers, Kevin, wanted to take me out to celebrate my promotion. We visited a nearby establishment for liquid libations. I asked if he wanted to invite the other assistant managers and he said "no," because he also wanted to ask my advice about something. When Kevin started to talk he had an atypical tone in his voice. He went on to tell me that he owed me an apology and that he felt extremely bad about what he had done. As I listened intently, he went on to tell me that he had intentionally taken $50 out of the restaurant's petty cash in the safe and put it back the next day. "What! Why?" I asked. By now he had tears in his eyes as he told me that the word had come down to "put that !@%* through the wringer." He wanted to see if I would follow cash procedures or whether I would take the money out of my own pocket to make things balance. When I asked why was he telling me this now, he said he had come to respect and admire me and that he did not want that guilt to forever haunt him. I told him I forgave him because I truly believed he was sincere.

After Kevin regained his composure we talked about what he wanted to do with the rest of his life, because although he was good at his job at the restaurant he was not really happy, and he did not look forward to a career in the restaurant business. He had never told anyone at BK this for fear that he might be fired, but he felt he could trust me. After asking him a few probing questions *(ask the right questions),* it turned out that he had always wanted to be a stockbroker. When I asked why he had never pursued it he admitted that he was a little scared of the risk. I encouraged him to go for it while he was still young enough, single enough, and smart enough to do it. He said that after seeing what I gave up to pursue a new career he was inspired to give it a shot. Two years later I was still the RVP of the Philadelphia region when I received a call from Kevin. He had become a licensed stockbroker.

ONE STEP AHEAD

"How can ten operating regions of the same company, selling the same product, using the same operations procedures, the same marketing and advertising programs, the same pricing structure, the same franchising requirements, and the same headquarters' corporate infrastructure produce such dramatically different operating results?" This was the question I pondered when I found out that I was going to the Philadelphia region as the Vice President and Regional General Manager (RVP).

My new boss told me that the Philly region was the most underperforming region in the company. Mystery shopper operations scores were consistently low, the morale of the people in the region was low, the attitude of many of the franchisees was bad, and the region had not achieved its profit plan in several years. My job was to reverse these trends, especially the "profit plan" part *(focus).*

Unlike the organization I inherited as Vice President of Systems and Services, this organization would require some major personnel changes. The organizational structure consisted of four operations area managers, and four department directors of marketing, human resources, development, and accounting. Within the first 12 months I had to replace four of my eight direct reports. Although it was real clear where I needed to focus my attention when I became Vice President of Systems and Services, it was not immediately clear where I needed to focus *most* when I took over as RVP.

First of all, I had a new set of "customers" that I did not have when running my first Burger King unit...franchisees. Nearly 350 of the 450 units were franchise owned and operated, and as soon as a region gets a new RVP they all want to lobby the new guy for more site approvals. If that did not work, they would open up "old wounds" about how they had been mistreated in the past and they just wanted to be treated fairly. Fortunately, 80 percent of my franchisees were not whiners, but the 20 percent who were wanted 80 percent of my time and that of my staff. It was also fortunate that my Director of Development, Jim Walsh, had been around a long time and was also one of my most competent and reliable people for sound advice. With Jim's help we were able to make a lot of our franchise customers happy at least temporarily, and neutralize most of those attitudes which were just "bad." In short order they were introduced to the happy B.E.E. philosophy, where in this case the "B" stood for "bad moods stay away."

Since the Philly region had such a high percentage of franchise units, obtaining consensus on marketing programs was a major task. The Burger King Corporate marketing function would develop the national marketing strategy and the supporting advertising and promotional vehicles. They would also provide a host of alternatives which could be executed at the regional level but consistent with the national campaign. For example, the national campaign might be advertising "combination meals" of sandwich, fry and drink, where the region could select the whopper combo or the burger combo with or without a price point, and buy additional local media to support the program. It was also possible to be running a marketing program at the regional level that did not tie directly to the timing of the national promotion. That's when you would see and hear that little disclaimer at the end of a commercial, "at participating restaurants." It just meant that not all the franchisees would agree. Company restaurants did not get the choice.

Marketing became a major area of my attention *(focus)*. More often than not we had to have the disclaimer, which diluted the impact of the message and subsequently produced sub-par sales results. We were able to convince most of our franchisees that it was costing all of us money by constantly going against the tide in "row boats" instead of with the tide in a "battleship." We did it with old-fashioned one-on-one common sense communications with as many people as we could, rather than the "because I say so" principle, which does not work. Pretty soon, the region's comparable sales started to be positive.

To sustain this trend, I knew even before I arrived at the region that operations would have to be more consistent and the service in the restaurants would have to be several notches higher, based on my experience in the Minneapolis region. Although most of the restaurants were operating according to "by the book" standards, there was little enthusiasm from the heart. What better way to move service up than with…"happy B.E.E.s."

It was my first application of the "happy B.E.E." culture for an entire region of 450 company and franchise restaurants. Trying to apply it directly in one unit is a lot different than applying it in 450 units, through multiple layers of operations management and multiple franchise ownerships…but it worked!

Our region mystery shopper's scores and our comparable sales started to rise even more. As I mentioned earlier, nothing inspires an organization like a victory. People were beginning to feel good about themselves again, working as a "battleship" going with the tide.

Better communications, improved operations, more consistent marketing, and high morale produced a fiscal year which exceeded the profit plan…convincingly! The Philly region exceeded the profit plan the following year also. Soon, many of my RVP counterparts were coming to visit me to see what was going on in my region. And as one RVP told me after his visit, "This is not the same Philly region. You seem to be *one step ahead* of everybody these days."

JUDAS AND THE HANGING

Not surprisingly, not everyone was thrilled that the Philly region was *one step ahead* and doing so well. Two specific instances were brought to my attention, which I call the "Judas" incident and the "hanging."

Despite the uncontestable performance of the region after nearly two and a half years as RVP, one of my direct reports took it upon himself to meet secretly with my boss. This was not the same boss that I worked for initially, but someone else who came into the position following a corporate organizational restructuring. "Judas" had been in his position when I arrived to take over the Philadelphia region and on the surface seemed supportive and was doing an adequate job. After meeting with "Judas," my boss found no basis to the accusation that "Herman is ruining the region," so he told me of the conversation.

I met with "Judas" and gave him two choices…resign or resign, because if he forced me to fire him it would not be an "honorable discharge." He resigned that day.

About a year later he called and asked to meet with me and I agreed. He apologized for what he had done and admitted that in retrospect he was wrong and did not know why he had taken such a risk. Although I could never substantiate my theory, I suspected later his reasons were related to the "hanging" incident.

Following one of Burger King's national conventions I was notified that there was a realignment of the regions which report to the divisional executive vice presidents. My new boss would be Bill DeLeat, who I knew but with whom I had not worked directly. He spent three days in Philly with me evaluating my operations from top to bottom. Each department director presented an update on their respective area, we visited a number of our company restaurants during the busy lunch and dinner periods, and we visited several of my franchisees and their operations…those in the 80 percent group.

After three intensive and enjoyable days with Bill, we had dinner together his last night in town. The two previous evenings we invited members of my staff so he could get better acquainted with them, but he told me specifically that he wanted the last dinner to be one-on-one.

During our discussion over dinner, he said that he had been thoroughly impressed with my operations, my people, and everything he had seen. This was his first time visiting the region, and he said it was nothing like its old reputation. He said it was also nothing like the image that was currently being "painted" of the region and me at headquarters. I said, "Please explain."

Bill told me that there were a lot of people that did not like me and wanted me fired. Thinking that I had done a pretty good job with the region based on its results, I was shocked. He went on to say that at the recent national convention several unhappy franchisees had bitterly complained to my old boss and several other corporate executives that I had to go because I was "ruining the region" (Does that sound familiar?). Because there was no hard evidence that I was ruining the region, it was decided to have me report to Bill so he could make an independent assessment. Up until that point I was almost "hung" without a trial based on hearsay and someone who did not want to see me succeed.

Bill worked very hard with some success to change that negative perception of the region and me, but when you are trying to change perception from negative to positive it is an uphill battle. When you are trying to change perception from positive to negative (as my invisible enemies were doing) it is a downhill ride.

Ironically, when there was speculation that corporate management might establish a third division with another divisional executive vice president, most of my RVP colleagues expressed opinions that I was the obvious choice, even though I was not looking for the job. I was, in fact, interviewed for the job, but a decision was made to not establish the third division…I never knew why.

Through it all, I continued to *focus* on my job and the Philadelphia region continued to stay "one step ahead."

DID YOU SAY PRESIDENT?

In March of 1986, I was attending an RVP meeting in San Francisco with Burger King's corporate management when someone brought me a note that said, "call Jeff." This was my boss' boss' boss, and the same Jeff Campbell that became President of Burger King Corporation when I started the fast-track program. Jeff was now Executive Vice President of the Restaurant Division for Pillsbury.

I immediately left the meeting and went to call Jeff at his office in Miami. I had no idea what he wanted because we had not talked in quite a while, given his much expanded responsibilities. I went to my hotel room to make the call to keep "inquiring ears" from being tempted.

His secretary answered and said Jeff was expecting my call so she put me right through. After some small talk about the weather in San Francisco and the RVP meeting, he told me that he needed to make a management change at Godfather's Pizza. He asked me how much I knew about Godfather's, and I said that I only knew that Pillsbury had acquired it as part of the acquisition of Diversifoods the previous August (1985), but I knew nothing about the company or the pizza business.

This call took place on a Wednesday and he wanted to know where I was going on Friday following the RVP meeting. I informed him that I was going downhill skiing in Colorado with some other RVPs. He then asked if I would stop in Miami to talk with him on my way to Colorado. We both laughed, knowing that Miami was certainly not "on the way" to Colorado from San Francisco. He then asked if I would change my plans because he wanted to talk to me about being President of Godfather's.

I said, "Did you say *President*?" He responded affirmatively.

I returned to my meeting obviously unable to concentrate, and to make matters worse, Jeff had asked me not to mention the subject to anyone before we talked on Friday. When my boss asked what Jeff had wanted I told him he wanted to talk to me about what it was like living in Minneapolis and working directly for Bill Spoor, since he would be moving to Pillsbury Corporate Headquarters. I also told my boss that I had advised Jeff to never force Bill Spoor to say "no," and to please not ask him about those !@%* letters in the atrium of the World Headquarters building.

CHAPTER 3

GET ON THE WAGON OR GET OUT OF THE WAY ... GODFATHER'S PIZZA, INC. FIGHTS BACK

Stranger in a Strange Land

First Sixty Days

Tactical Action Plan (F'87)

OVERVIEW

All Systems Meeting—May 29, 1986

Big Value

Where's the Celebration Party?

Leveraged Buy Out

Godfather's Pizza, Inc.—1988 Convention

It's Working

"THERE IS NO JOY IN EASY SAILING"

"There is no thrill in easy sailing
When the skies are clear and blue.
There is no joy in merely doing
Things which anyone can do.
But there is some satisfaction
That is mighty sweet to take,
When you reach a destination
That you thought you'd never make."

Spirella

Stranger in a Strange Land

I arrived in Omaha, Nebraska, on April 1, 1986 as the new President of Godfather's Pizza, Inc. (GPI). In 1985, The Pillsbury Company acquired GPI as part of its acquisition of Diversifoods, Inc., which had acquired GPI in 1983. Pillsbury was primarily interested in acquiring the nearly 300 Burger King units which Diversifoods owned and operated, but they would not sell the BK units without GPI as part of the deal. Neither Pillsbury nor Diversifoods wanted to keep GPI because of its negative growth and declining sales, which produced declining profitability (Exhibit 3-1), as well as the large number of pending litigations against GPI.

I had never been to Omaha or Nebraska, and I was new to the pizza business. I declined Jeff's offer to accompany me to GPI head-quarters on my first day, because I wanted to minimize the perceived "fanfare" of a formal arrival, and I wanted to experience my new job as an adventure.

When I arrived at the corporate office, I was shown to a waiting room outside of my soon-to-be office, since my predecessor had not yet removed all of his personal items. It's not like he did not know I was coming; we had met in Jeff's office the week before. We were to have a short orientation meeting. While waiting to meet with my pre-decessor, I met my new Executive Assistant, Jan, and the Executive Vice President of Corporate Support, Ron Gartlan. Ron would even-tually become my business partner in putting together a Leveraged Buy Out (LBO) of GPI twenty months later.

While waiting for my orientation meeting, I wandered over to the employee lunch facility to get some juice and maybe a doughnut. When I walked into the lunch room, only one other person was there

Exhibit 3-1 *Godfather's Pizza Inc., Sales and Growth Decline*

	F'84	*F'86*
Number of Restaurants	911	671
System Sales ($ millions)	311	265
Average Sales/Unit ($ thousands)	395	360

and we politely spoke to each other. As I was getting some juice, she asked, "Are you new here?" I replied, "Yes, I'm Herman Cain and this is my first day." She said, "Hi, I'm Lori Williams and I work in accounts receivable." Lori then asked me, "What will you be doing...What's your job?" I replied, "I'm the new president of the company." Lori then said, "I have heard every line in the book, but this is a new one...you are president of the company...get out of here, who are you trying to kid?" We both laughed and then she said, "It's nice meeting you. I've got to get back to work...see you around." I said, "OK."

Later that afternoon Ron Gartlan called an employee meeting to introduce me to everyone who worked in the corporate office. After a brief introduction by Ron, I made some comments to the group. As I started to speak I noticed someone sitting on the last row of the auditorium, trying not to be seen by hiding behind the person sitting in front of her. I leaned to one side to see who it was, and it was Lori! After reciting "There Is No Joy In Easy Sailing" by Spirella to get everyone's attention, I said "Hi Lori." Everyone seemed surprised that I knew Lori since this was my first day, so I explained to the audience what had happened that morning. Obviously, everyone thought the story was hilarious...everyone except Lori. By the time the laughter quieted down, though, Lori also found the incident amusing. I then announced to Lori that she was going to be famous, because I would never forget that conversation and that I would tell it often. I could tell that the audience liked my sense of humor, which took the edge off of what could have been a very stark and overly serious introduction.

During that first meeting I talked about my background, my career, my experiences, and some of my philosophies. The most important point I made during that meeting was that I did not come to GPI as president with the notion that I had all the answers. In fact, they and others that I would talk to had the answers to GPI's future success, and my job was to help formulate what they knew into an action plan, and then do it.

I also informed the group that I would not have come to GPI if I did not believe it could be successful again. This belief was based on my discussion with Jeff Campbell about the job and the challenge, and the excitement of the possibility of success, rather than the possibility of failure. The pizza segment was still growing, the restaurant industry was growing, and GPI had a great product when it was executed correctly. Something was missing.

After the meeting, I met with my predecessor where we discussed several issues which he thought needed immediate attention. He talked about the F'86 financial results, which were going to be bad (I thought to myself, with two months to go there's not much that can be done about that, and I was fresh out of miracles), setting up reserve funds for company units that needed to be closed, our soft drink supplier contract, dissatisfaction in the franchisee community, product research, and briefly the people. I found it odd that he did not talk about QSC (quality, service, and cleanliness) or operations. Everything I had learned at my first restaurant manager's job and as RVP of the Philadelphia region suggested that QSC is everything! If an operation is not consistent in QSC, the question is not if you will go out of business, the question is when. This was the first sign that the "right questions" had not been asked, and the right problems may not have been identified.

At the end of our meeting, which turned out to be brief, I thanked him again and wished him well. (Finally, I could get my office...I had work to do!)

Ron Gartlan, Executive Vice President, and I had dinner together that evening after a long, exciting first day at GPI. My adrenaline was still pretty high over just being there, so I was not yet starting to feel tired. Our discussion was direct and honest no matter how sensitive the issue. In fact, I recall Ron prefacing the answer to one of my questions with "I don't know if you are going to keep me around, but I'm going to tell you the truth anyway." By this point in our discussion, I knew that Ron was a person I wanted to keep on my team because he was not only knowledgeable about the business and the company, but most importantly, he came across as extremely trustworthy. Ron had been with GPI since 1982, when the original founder of the company still owned and ran GPI, and had been a key player in both the public offering and the sale of the company to Diversifoods, Inc. He had seen just about everything that had happened to GPI, including the parade of four presidents in three years that had "touched down" briefly at GPI.

During the remainder of my first week at GPI, I had one-on-one meetings with the top 20 people in the company. These discussions were extremely useful in helping me to understand why the business was declining, since many of the people I talked with had been with the company longer than the previous four presidents combined. These discussions also helped to identify what we needed to do to get GPI moving in the right direction again. Although each person answered the question "If I were President of GPI" a little differently, they all expressed the need for focus, consistency, and leadership. In none of the discussions did we specifically talk about what they meant by leadership, but they all alluded to the fact that they would know it when they saw it, but had not seen it lately at Godfather's.

Another consistent message I received from the one-on-one's was a sense that the existing management group strongly believed in the

Godfather's Pizza concept and that it could indeed be successful again. Some of the specific ideas about how this could be achieved included:

"We need a customer-focus awareness"

"Franchisees will not be resistant to direction, leadership, and standardization" *(I had been told by my predecessor that they would be resistant.)*

"Standardize our training system (training by the slice) and make it available *free* to the franchisees, then require implementation" *(I could not imagine charging extra for the training system in the first place.)*

"Develop pizza by the slice or pizza buffet for lunch"

"The total system today is fragmented...not bonding"

"Develop marketing programs for adaptability to each market"

"Our system at the restaurant level does not allow a manager to succeed"

"Focus priorities for management team"

"Focus on operational excellence"

"Test home delivery full-scale in our Seattle market" *(Seattle was and still is our largest market.)*

"Develop who we are to be"

"Establish marketing consistency"

"Focus objectives and stick to them"

"Solid leadership, communications, and focus"

"Too many fire drills"

"Weekend working in the restaurant every six months should be mandatory for management...to avoid "ivory tower-itis.""

"We have not been able to kill Godfather's"

...and many, many more.

A picture was evolving very rapidly in my head from over 20 hours of listening to people closest to the situation.

I also visited several GPI restaurants and met several of the franchisees based in Omaha. Some were courteous, friendly, and constructive with their feedback about what needed to be done, and some were downright rude and hostile.

Franchising systems such as GPI typically succeed by achieving economies of scale, maintaining a consistent identity, and working collectively to combat competition. But many of the people who became franchisees of GPI had done so during a time when the growth rate in the pizza segment and the restaurant industry tolerated more inconsistent operations and could still make money. Times had definitely changed by 1986, when competition was more intense, Godfather's identify had become blurred, and operational consistency was nonexistent. Company and franchise operations had to achieve some bonding to be successful again, as several of my management people pointed out.

That same entrepreneurial spirit *(E-factor)* that causes someone to want to run their own business (by becoming a franchisee of a business concept) is that same spirit that causes them to want to be different at times from the system and do it their own way. *Success requires a balance.*

One of my most encouraging discussions occurred the first week on the job, when I met John Chisholm and Jim Morrissey, who at that time were our second largest franchise operation with 33 restaurants. Ron took me to meet them at their 76th and Pacific Street restaurant, where they showed me around, told me about their operation, and we got acquainted. John and Jim were also among the few operators who were still profitable despite GPI's problems, so their perspective was particularly important in shaping a turnaround plan.

They talked about a lot of things that needed to be done, including many of the issues my one-on-one discussions had revealed. But the most important comment I remember from that conversation was, "you may have to require us to do some things we do not want to do

Exhibit 3-2   *ONE-ON-ONE FEEDBACK—A Synopsis*

Existing People	. . . . Good
Strategic and Tactical Focus	. . . . Non-existent
Infrastructure	. . . . Weak
Corporate and Field Morale	. . . . Poor
Franchisees	. . . . Hopeful
Godfather's Identity	. . . . Blurred
Leadership and Decisiveness	. . . . Weak

no executive running those functions, but I was able to fill the positions almost immediately. It did not take me long to "redirect" the careers of four vice presidents for various reasons. One of them lacked focus, two of them were in the wrong job, and one demonstrated that I could not trust him...he was telling me one thing, and telling the people in his department something different. This was certainly not the culture I wanted to establish because it created a barrier to motivation instead of removing one. So I removed him.

The weakest management area was clearly operations because of inconsistencies in the restaurants and a lack of enthusiasm of the restaurant managers and crew. I attributed much of this to "too many bosses" trying to run operations—an executive vice president of operations, a vice president of company operations, a vice president of franchise operations, several regional vice presidents of company operations, area managers, district managers, and finally, the person running the restaurant...the manager. Today we have two operations vice presidents (east and west) reporting to the chief operating officer.

The strongest executive was Ron Gartlan, who was in charge of planning, procurement, administration, personnel, and all other support functions. Ron was thoughtful, analytical, responsive, and *bru-*

for the good of the system." That comment inspired me because it meant they understood that times had changed and that we had to become a system, and to do so the franchisor had to *lead*.

Today John and Jim are our largest franchise operation with 68 Godfather's Pizza restaurants, and still one of the most successful!

It had been a long and exciting week getting to know GPI and its people, and I decided to remain in town over the weekend rather than go back to Philadelphia, in order to get acquainted with the city and reflect on what I had heard and seen that first week. I was beginning to feel less and less like a "stranger in a strange land."

First Sixty Days

When I accepted the job as President of GPI, my boss, Jeff Campbell, asked me to develop a 100-day plan to determine our turnaround strategy. The feedback I received during my first week proved critical to that strategy and allowed us even to accelerate its creation (Exhibit 3-2). That feedback also helped me establish where I would focus my attention during the first 60 days.

My initial assessment of the existing management people was better than I had expected in some departments, but weaker in others. The "keepers" showed many of the "three plus three" qualities in what they discussed and how they discussed it during the one-on-one meetings, whereas the weaker players displayed lack of clarity and focus in the discussions. I had already decided that a wholesale "house cleaning" of the entire management team would not be prudent, because I needed a core group of key people as fast as possible who could respond to my way of doing things…fast, focused, and friendly.

The marketing, development, and human resources functions had *tally honest...*if you asked him. During that first 60 days I asked him about a lot of things, especially his perspective on many of the existing people.

Gary Batenhorst was (and still is) the general counsel handling the many litigations facing GPI, and there were many. Even though Pillsbury's legal department had advised me to bring in a "heavyweight" attorney (preferably from Pillsbury) to work with Gary to resolve the lawsuits, I decided not to do so because after reviewing each case with Gary and Ron, I felt that they were well under control. Fourteen months later all the lawsuits had been resolved...Gary turned out to be our "heavy-weight" attorney.

When the dust settled, four executives were retained as part of my executive team, three new people were hired, and four were "redirected." My new team abounded in entrepreneurial spirit *(E-factor)*, which often made my job as leader even more challenging. But I would rather have more than less, because it gives you more choices to select the right alternative. The common thread on my new team, however, was a "can-do" attitude.

The non-existence of strategic and tactical focus was no surprise, since the revolving door of GPI presidents did not leave any of them in place long enough to establish a strategy or focus. Being outsized by our three largest competitors with 4,500, 2,800, and 900 units respectively, and having read *Marketing Warfare* by Ries and Trout, the issue of *focus* was top of mind with me.

During a meeting with the field operations management, I asked a series of questions to help determine just what our strategic focus should be, and to start the process of getting the whole organization focused. To a group of about 60 operations district managers and some vice presidents I asked, "If I say Pizza Hut to you what comes to mind?" Several of the responses were, "red roofs, biggest competitor, all things to all people, deep pockets," and so on. These were all valid responses. I then asked, "If I say Domino's to you what comes to mind?," and several people responded almost in unison, "delivery," also an appropriate response about the second largest competitor in our segment. When I asked, "What does Little Caesars bring to mind?," the responses were "two for one and low price." I then asked, "When I say Godfather's Pizza what comes to mind?" There was silence. I then asked, "Well, what did Godfather's used to stand for?" Finally someone said in a hesitant voice, "quality."

If my own people were uncertain about our identity, then communicating our identity to our customers would be an even more difficult task. This little Q&A exercise also confirmed what someone had said during my first week of one-on-one meetings, that Godfather's had a blurred image. I expected as much in the minds of our customers, but not in the minds of my own people! We had some work to do.

I then suggested to the group that we *refocus* on quality, since that is what helped to make Godfather's successful in the first place. There were some gentle nods of agreement. In fact, attribute ratings obtained from a consumer survey had confirmed that despite some inconsistent execution, Godfather's overall rating, good taste, and product quality perceptions were still very high relative to its two largest competitors (Exhibit 3-3). I then suggested that rather than trying to be the "biggest," we should just be the "best"...a few more nods of agreement. Instead of trying to deliver faster than Domino's, let's be the best pizza when it gets there. Instead of trying to be the cheapest, let's give customers the best value for their money. By now there were more nods and even some smiles that this was beginning to make sense. After going through a series of examples, I then challenged all departments to develop plans indicating how we could reestablish "quality" as our niche in the minds of pizza customers, but most importantly, in the minds of our own people. Earlier, someone had made the comment that, "we have not been able to kill Godfather's;" we were now going to find out if this was true.

A focus on quality requires consistent execution; it does not make

Exhibit 3-3 *Attribute Ratings—Top 2 Box* (Seattle)*

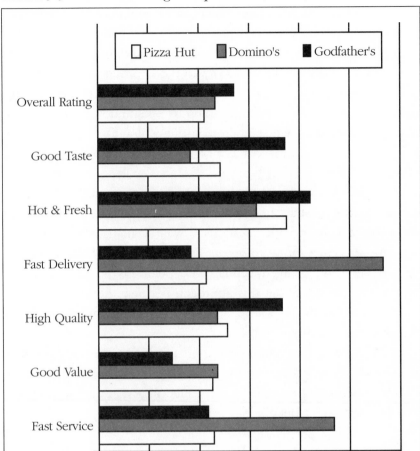

☐ Pizza Hut   ▨ Domino's   ■ Godfather's

* On a Scale of 0–10; 0 = Poor, 10 = Favorable

sense to build one perfect pizza. We had designed our infrastructure to come as close as humanly possible on every pizza. Now, having a clear focus on quality, priorities for marketing, product research, new unit development, training, operations, and all respective departmental functions, consistent quality could be maintained more effectively and productively.

For example, the training department would establish the TBTS (Training by the Slice) system as its top priority because it was critical to driving consistency of execution in the restaurants. And rather than having to adapt the TBTS system to many different menu variations, they needed to adapt it only to those products that we were going to refocus our menu on...Godfather's original crust pizza. This did not mean that we were not going to pursue new product variations, but only after we standardized our ability to deliver our flagship product, and in the context of always being able to make the best pizza...first.

As discussion in this field operations meeting started to open up, it became obvious that there was no lack of ideas. But as I continued to probe the group with questions it was clear that the concept of *focusing on fewer things to accomplish more* was a little difficult at first. By the end of the meeting, the operations people were cautiously enthusiastic about this approach because they had been the ones most directly responsible for trying to implement too many things in the restaurants too fast.

It did not take long for the entire organization to begin to resonate this idea of focus. In fact, by the end of April (my first month on the job) we had pulled together our first tactical action plan to reinvigorate our "quality" reputation.

Morale began to pick up immediately in the corporate office and in field operations as we started to communicate specifics about the tactical action plan. The excitement did not come from a host of new ideas in the plan, because most of them had been afloat throughout the three years of performance decline at GPI. The excitement came from being given specific direction to execute certain ideas. I gave the go-ahead to do the Seattle delivery test even before I had approval for capital from the parent company *(E-factor)*. It was a relatively small amount of capital dollars, but by the time we would have gotten through the formal approval process we could have developed and implemented the system...and we did.

We established a pizza by the slice ("hot slice") project development team and put the project on a fast track. The initial rollout date was September 1986, but we took the risk of accelerating it to August. *An accelerated fast-track project can be very effective in getting the organization to focus because it leaves little time to be distracted.* This project required new portioning specifications, new equipment, a new marketing campaign with advertising, promotions, and in-store point-of-purchase materials, a training module...everything from A to Z except a good pizza, which we already had. We just needed to develop a way to cut the pizzas in equal slices since they were going to be sold by the slice.

These initiatives created a sense of decisiveness and direction. People instinctively like to win and succeed, and they know they can't do that if they do not start. As Will Rogers said, "Even if you are on the right tracks, you'll get run over if you just sit there."

Ron had suggested that I be visible because people can be inspired when they see and hear directly from the leader. Needless to say, I was everywhere spreading the focus message and challenging people for even more ideas about how we could win again. At the same time, this allowed me to gain even more insight about the pizza business, GPI, and its strengths and weaknesses. The more I learned, the more my own morale was enhanced.

We developed a logo (see the insert) to distinguish our new attitude from the old paradigm, which we also used as a constant reminder to ourselves of the underlying principles of our strategy and tactics...*focus*. We initiated a monthly newsletter entitled (what else) *Focus* for everyone in the GPI system. The *focus* logo appeared on T-shirts, caps, paperweights, marketing plans, and everywhere imaginable as a symbol of how we had to think in order to survive against much larger competitors.

The "guerrilla warfare" notion was used to communicate a sense of urgency about how we had to compete, and to denote the principles used by the successful competitive underdogs described by Ries and Trout:

> LET THE LEADERS LEAD...with expensive and risky new product innovations. Then look for "halo" opportunities.
>
> ATTACK "NICHES"...which reduce the size of your battleground.
>
> FOCUS RESOURCES...to achieve greatest impact with a small arsenal of competitive weapons.

This also helped to create a corporate mindset that we could win again, using "guerrilla" tactics without being the big "gorilla." Winning is the biggest boost to morale there is.

Although Godfather's product quality perception had survived executional abuses, our marketing and advertising image had not survived a serious "blurring." That first operations meeting proved this, as did my own impressions of creative materials I had reviewed.

The original Godfather's registered trademark (see the color insert) was not clear to me at first because I did not understand the graphic in front of the word pizza. After it was explained to me that it was a hand from a pinstriped suit holding a pizza, I understood. But then I asked my marketing people, "Are we going to explain it to every customer so they understand the graphic?" *(ask the right questions)*. Obviously, they responded, "no."

I then reviewed the most recent television and radio commercials, which had been done by a well-respected advertising agency. The tag line was, "Godfather's Pizza, find one, it's worth it." My impression was a negative one because the tag line highlighted a negative rather than a positive, namely, "we do not have a lot of units like the other guys, but if you can find us, we promise it will be good." I have always believed in accentuating the positive. I may have been a bit impulsive but based on what I saw, the opinion of the marketing staff, and the opinion of "Mr. Brutally Honest"…I fired the agency.

We concluded that the old trademark had started to look dated and decided to develop a new one. Not wanting to be accused of being totally impulsive on every decision and with something as important as our registered trademark, I hired an outside agency to develop proposals for a new logo with new colors. Since we were suffering from blurred identity, I wanted us to go forward with a fresh, clean new look more consistent with a company with a new attitude. After several months of analysis and evaluation, we selected our current logo (see the insert), which has served us well to date.

The new logo not only gave us a more effective and memorable identity for our customers and external constituencies, it also served as a symbolic separation from GPI's most recent past. We needed to build momentum fast and when we did, I did not want the organization to be subconsciously drawn back into its old way of thinking.

Most of the franchise community was very receptive to our management changes, agency change, our *focus* strategy, changes to improve our identity, and the projects we immediately undertook to revitalize GPI. Many of our franchisees had been in the system during its hey-day (1973-1983) and had grown severely disappointed and discouraged by the events of the previous two and a half years.

Many of our franchise owners were cautiously hopeful that, first of all, I would be in the job for more than a few months and, secondly, that I would do something. They also continued to believe in the Godfather's concept but realized we needed to become a system. They wanted to believe that TPC was committed to giving GPI a chance to succeed but it was a wait-and-see belief. They were hopeful, but happy days were not here again…yet. They and the corporate staff were hopeful that I was the leader they needed.

Thirty days into my new job as President of GPI I presented our tactical action plan to my boss for F'87, which started June 1, 1986. The plan had come together much faster than originally anticipated in my "100-day plan" because of the wealth of ideas, enthusiasm, and energy just waiting to be focused, prioritized, and inspired. The bottom line of what I learned that first 30 days is summed up in the overview I wrote for the plan . . .

Tactical Action Plan (F'87)

OVERVIEW

During the last two and one-half years, Godfather's Pizza, Inc. has experienced merger, acquisition, and excessive turnover in top management, while simultaneously attempting the transition from an entrepreneurial company to a more structured company. This period of instability has been traumatic to the Godfather's system, which has produced a blurred vision of its identity, direction, and capabilities, resulting in declining sales and profitability. This decline in performance, while our segment of the industry has enjoyed a generous growth rate, accentuates the urgency to demonstrate the short- and long-term profitability of the Godfather's Pizza business.

This plan outlines a focused vision of our identity, direction, and capabilities, which will allow us to revive Godfather's Pizza during the critical twelve months of F'87. Beyond F'87, our objective is to enhance the profitability of Godfather's Pizza, Inc., such that we consistently meet or exceed expectations.

Our objectives (Exhibit 3-4) for that first full fiscal year of my presidency seemed aggressive relative to the recent trend, but we felt that with some luck, they were attainable. More importantly, they were

Exhibit 3-4 *Godfather's Pizza, Inc., F'87, Objectives*

- Achieve comparable sales increases of 10 percent for company stores and 5 percent for franchised stores.

- Restore product quality and consistency throughout the system.

- Improve the system average QSC from 79 percent to 85 percent.

- Develop and roll out a market-wide pizza delivery system in the Seattle market.

- Open the required number of delivery-only units to support market-wide delivery in Seattle.

- Develop an overall business infrastructure for the Godfather's system.

"Establish Winning Momentum"

tangible, specific, and measurable, which would provide good benchmarks of our progress to the entire organization. The management team and I were so enthused about the plan and the projects we had initiated that we wanted to share it with more of our operations people, our franchisees and their people, as well as with our suppliers of ingredients, goods, and services.

I suggested an all-system meeting, which we held on May 29, nearly 60 days after my start date. We selected that date because the summer months were generally not good times for maximum attendance. Secondly, most people wanted to know what was "the new guy" up to, and if we waited until September much of what we had decided to do would be old news. Additionally, I wanted to meet our people and our franchisees sooner rather than later.

The turnout for the meeting was tremendous. I gave an extended opening presentation of our focus, plans, projects, and priorities, as well as what they could expect from us as a new leadership team and what we expected of them. I emphasized that GPI, the franchisor, would in fact lead, and that we would be very flexible on a lot of specific issues facing each franchise owner. However, I also emphasized that there were three things we absolutely would not negotiate on— quality standards, operations standards, and the obligation for them to "pay us our money." Delinquent payment of franchise fees had reached an all-time high, and I did not want us to be unnecessarily distracted. Those that were committed to our prospects for success responded positively to the new direction, and those that were not committed did not respond positively so we eventually "redirected" their association with GPI.

That presentation was followed by presentations of specifics by major functional areas (marketing, development, operations, research, training, etc.), presented by the respective person in charge. I required extensive preparation and practice for the presentations, because you only get one chance to make a first impression. I closed the day-long program with one of the most inspiring speeches I have ever given. This was the opinion of those in attendance.

All Systems Meeting—May 29, 1986

Over the last two days we have brought you up to date on what has happened during the first 60 days of a new beginning. These 60 days have redefined our direction for the next 60 months. Therefore, a final challenge is in order.

As such, I want to challenge each of you to do three things which will change our individual and collective futures if you choose to accept this call for action.

First, I challenge each of you to dream again. The turbulence of the last three years has dampened your ability to envision goals and achievements beyond the problems of the day.

The feelings you experienced when business was declining— while your competitor's performance was increasing—stifled your ability to creatively attack problems and turn them into opportunities.

Lack of focus and clarity has poisoned your desire to aspire for possibilities beyond your grasp.

We believe focus has been established. As we evolve out of our entrepreneurial state into a more stable and structured existence, we believe that our business can once again thrive and that turbulence has now been replaced with order, direction, and positive intensity.

Therefore, I challenge you to dream again of possibilities beyond your grasp. I challenge you to dream of success, prosperity, and personal fulfillment once again. When you allow yourself to dream, you look at a mound of clay and see a masterpiece. You look at a glass of water half empty as a glass half filled. When you dream again, you are able to recognize that problems are merely dangerous opportunities that could unlock the doors to your success. When you dream again, you view today as the first day of the rest of your life. I challenge you to dream of Godfather's in 1990 as the number one pizza chain in the world. And if you truly do dream of being a part of that achievement, your creative energies will be unleashed and unstoppable. I challenge you to dream again about what Godfather's can become.

Secondly, I challenge each of you to commit yourself to the task before us, as others have already committed to your success.

Sixty days ago I came to Godfather's with a curiosity about what I would find. I had already accepted my newly bestowed responsibilities even before I stepped foot on Nebraska soil and before I met or knew anyone or anything about Godfather's. I also came 60 days ago with a 100-day plan as to how we would formulate a plan of action for the future. Sixty days ago, I came to Godfather's anxious to tackle a situation considered by some of our external constituencies to be irreversible. I came without a golden parachute because I never entertained the idea that the situation was irreversible. I came committed to prove the skeptics wrong because I have a personal, fundamental belief in the power of human determination. I came to Godfather's believing in you even before I met you. I challenge you to commit and believe in yourself and Godfather's Pizza as a system.

When I arrived at Godfather's Pizza on April 1st in 1986, I found that there were others who believed that victory could be ours. I found people who were not only personally committed but who also possessed ideas, skills, capabilities, and the tenacity necessary to accomplish the job ahead of us. Members of our management team and your own elected Franchise Advisory Council made it possible for us to achieve the 100-day plan in 25 days. Within the last 60 days about six months' of work has been completed—six months' work in 60 days because they shared the belief and commitment that we can and will succeed.

In addition, there are those like myself who have joined our effort knowing only that we would be engaged in a competitive fight for our lives and not knowing the magnitude of our ammunition or the severity of the enemy.

One of the questions asked by some franchisees during my early days at Godfather's was, "What is the commitment of Pillsbury?" Pillsbury's commitment is best summarized by what it could do but has not done. Namely, because of the relatively minimal financial investment in Godfather's, Pillsbury could eliminate Godfather's from its books as a tax write-off with a stroke of a bean-counter's pen and barely miss a step—if it so desired. But Pillsbury does not desire to do so. Obviously, Pillsbury's commitment is much greater than just dollars and cents.

I challenge you to commit yourself to the task before us as others have already committed to your success.

The third, and concluding, challenge to every Godfather's corporate employee, to every operator, to every owner, to every restaurant manager, to every crew member, to every person con-

nected in any way to the Godfather's system is to "Let's go." Let's get on with re-writing the currently anticipated future of Godfather's in the annals of the restaurant industry.

There are generally three kinds of people in the world. People who make things happen, people who watch things happen, and people who say, "What in the hell happened?"

People who make things happen—they dream. People who make things happen—they commit themselves. People who make things happen say, "Let's go."

If we are to be successful we must agree to listen to one another. We must agree to disagree with one another but agree to support and move with the majority as a system.

In the last two days we have described what we believed to be a start in the right direction. We do not know absolutely if it is 100 percent right, nor do we claim to have all the answers. But fact, logic, experience, collective thinking, and our gut tell us that it is at least 80 percent right, which, when added to 100 percent teamwork will produce 200 percent success...if we all say, "Let's go." We must, and will, be on a different timetable.

As one anonymous author wrote: "Life is just a minute—only 60 seconds in it. Forced upon me—can't refuse it. Didn't seek it. Didn't choose it. But it's up to me to use it. I must suffer if I lose it—give an account if I abuse it. Just a tiny little minute but eternity is in it."

I realize that this timetable may be too fast for some, and I realize that the objectives may be too aggressive for many. And I realize that the war we are about to wage may be too bloody and risky for some. But to paraphrase the motto of the U.S. Marine Corps, we are looking for a few good people. We will be successful with a few good people who have the inner vision to dream. We will be successful with a few good people who have the tenacity to commit. We will be successful with a few good people with the desire to aspire to make things happen by accepting the challenge to "Let's go."

Let's yank victory from the jaws of defeat!

People! People! People! Apart we are weak. Together we are strong.

In the unforgettable words of my grandfather, a Georgia farmer all his life, who would hitch a team of mules to the wagon on Saturdays for the weekly trip into the local town: "Them that's going—get on the wagon...them that ain't—get out of the way."

Them that's going—get on the wagon...them that ain't—get out of the way!

Big Value

Most people who attended that all systems meeting "got on the wagon." We had refocused our strategy. Product specifications and operational standards were being established and implemented. We had hired a new (different) advertising agency. We were developing a new corporate and advertising identity. Our franchisees were cautiously hopeful again. We had successfully rolled out the pizza by the slice ("hot slice") program for our lunch daypart. The pizza delivery test was moving forward in the Seattle market (our largest market). Morale throughout the system was very high. The management team had shown decisiveness and resumed its leadership role.

All of these initiatives were showing great promise of paying off, but it would be several months before some of these translated into increased sales. "Hot slice" had started to build our lunch business but we realized that it would build slowly over time, since consumer habits are hard to break and most lunch consumers were in the habit of going somewhere other than Godfather's for lunch.

One day in early September I called the Vice President of Research and Development to my office to talk about an idea I had that might give us a short-term sales boost while our other initiatives took effect. Since our product was a premium quality product at a premium price,

I wondered if we could develop a product variation that had great price appeal *without sacrificing our quality.* She asked how much appeal I wanted it to have and I said, "two large pizzas for $12 and we still make money." That sounded like a "big value," but I did not know if we could do it. She asked for a couple of days to work on it.

A few days later, I received a request to come to our product development kitchen to try the product. It was two large pizzas with the same quality ingredients proportioned differently, with a food cost that would allow us to make a decent margin. A pepperoni pizza and a four-topping pizza with plenty of toppings at a great price! Several of the other management team members were with me and they also liked the idea and the product, so we decided to try it in a few units with some in-store promotional materials.

After thinking about the idea for a few days and having tried the product, we decided to just go ahead and roll it out in as many of our restaurants as possible, such that the big "gorilla" would not have time to steal the idea and do it first with a lot more marketing weight behind it. Since we were more focused and this was still on strategy, we decided to just "go for it" *(E-factor).*

We quickly developed a marketing program to support the rollout and had the procedures operational by October in most of our restaurants. We were moving so fast on this that we just decided to call it "Big Value."

"Big Value" took off like a rocket! It gave customers who had not visited us in a while a compelling reason to stop by Godfather's. To say that it exceeded our expectations is an understatement. Restaurants had to order more pans to keep up with the demand during peak periods. We got complaints from restaurant managers that their ovens were not fast enough or big enough. What a nice problem to have! We solved the problem, and our restaurants were crowded during dinner again. By November many restaurants were hitting new sales records with double-digit comparable sales increases that they had not seen in years (Exhibit 3-5).

Exhibit 3-5 *'87 "Turnaround"—Godfather's Pizza, Inc.*

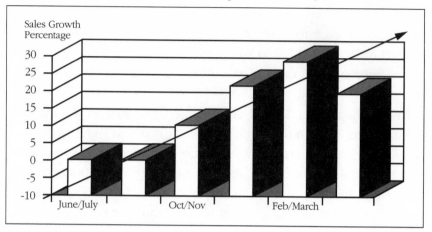

Many of our franchisees had also jumped on the "Big Value" wagon and were experiencing similar spectacular results. One of our largest franchise owners called and insisted on a meeting with me. He would not tell me what he wanted to discuss, so naturally I was suspicious. When we had met during my first 60 days, he didn't think much of this "focus" stuff and our plans.

When he arrived the next day, he came into my office with a small portable cassette tape player and asked me to please have a seat. He turned it on and the song "Happy Days Are Here Again" was on the tape. After the song played, he thanked me and got up and left. He just said "thanks, good-bye" and left. I guess that meant he was pleased with what was happening.

Obviously, "Big Value" created a lot of excitement because nothing boosts morale like positive sales increases, especially double-digit sales increases. However, we did not take our *focus* off our other initiatives, because the success of those would ensure that we could keep those customers who had rediscovered Godfather's.

Sometimes when you are trying for a base hit in baseball terms, it goes over the fence for a home run. This was just what we needed to put an exclamation point on our first year of the "turnaround."

Where's the Celebration Party?

The results of my first full year (F'87) as president of GPI exceeded all expectations. The pizza delivery test in Seattle was successful, restaurant operations had improved measurably, comparable sales for company-operated restaurants were up 10 percent versus a 12 percent decline the previous year, franchisee comparable sales were up 4 percent versus a 7 percent decline the previous year, and operating profit at the restaurant level went from 8.9 percent in F'86 to 13.2 percent in F'87, and *all* the lawsuits had been settled!

My management team was excited about our great performance year. We were also excited about our upcoming company long-range strategic plan presentation to our parent company, The Pillsbury Company. We just knew that after having such a great turnaround year that there would be more confidence in the long-term potential of GPI as a growth vehicle, since a large portion of its business portfolio at that time consisted of restaurant chains like Burger King, Bennigan's, Steak and Ale, and a Chinese fast food concept they were experimenting with called Quick Wok.

Ron and I worked very hard on putting together our strategic plan, which we presented in the fall of 1987 during TPC's and GPI's F'88. We requested capital to upgrade our restaurants to the new image we had developed, capital for new units primarily in existing profitable markets to improve our market penetration, and capital for new in-store point-of-sale equipment for better cash control and better information for labor scheduling and sales analysis.

In return, we projected that we could grow the sales, profit, and return on capital to TPC requirements. We realized that we only had one year of encouraging results, but we had to "crawl before we could walk or run." We strongly believed that it could be sustained with our strategy. Additionally, the pizza segment was the fastest growing quick-service restaurant segment in the industry, making GPI (we thought) a good candidate for growth.

After the presentation to TPC top management, Ron and I returned to our Minneapolis hotel and had dinner in one of the hotel restaurants. We decided to treat ourselves to the fine dining restaurant, since we felt the presentation had gone extremely well. During dinner Ron and I decided it was rather strange that no one offered to take us to dinner after such a great year and such a great presentation, or that there was no celebration party being thrown in our honor.

As we discussed the reactions, comments, questions, and even the body language during the presentation, we both started to get the feeling that GPI's days were numbered as a subsidiary of TPC. After having achieved what some people called a "miracle" in just 14 months, it appeared that it had nothing to do with the decision to keep or sell GPI.

We decided that evening that if TPC were planning to sell us off, that we would wait and let them bring up the issue. We then got a really crazy idea. If they did decide to sell GPI, then *we* would buy it. I asked Ron if he had ever dreamed of doing something like that and he said, "nope." I said, "Neither have I, but how hard can it be, I've bought a house before." We would soon find out just how hard it was. That momentous discussion with Ron that evening would prove to be another historic turning point for GPI.

Leveraged Buy Out

Over the next four months we did not receive approval for any of the major capital we had requested, so we knew something was cooking and it wasn't just the pizza. In January of 1988, I received a call from Jerry Levin, the Executive Vice President of Acquisitions and Divestitures for TPC, who wanted to have a meeting with us in Minneapolis. I was visiting our restaurants in Seattle at the time of the call, so I changed my itinerary so that we could go see him. Ron met me in Minneapolis.

When we met with Jerry the next day, he officially informed us that (surprise) TPC had decided to sell Godfather's. We were shocked and astounded...NOT! He then wanted to know if the management had an interest in buying GPI, and I told him we would get back to him in a few days.

Ron and I had already made that decision months earlier following our strategic plan presentation, but Jerry was the guy we would have to negotiate with so we had to stay "cool" and not appear overly excited. About two weeks later we negotiated a purchase price, and then we had to "achieve the desired results"...make the deal happen. As it turned out, Jerry actually helped us to make the deal happen, drawing upon his many years of experience in doing deals for TPC. But getting the deal done was no easy task given GPI's recent turbulent financial history.

With the assistance of an outside consultant on leveraged buy outs, we put together our presentation for potential lending institutions, and then the work really began. We presented our story to nearly 20 potential banks and lending institutions, each presentation being a half to three-quarters of a day in length. Each bank brought a team of people who would often try to put us in a "crossfire" of questions, but Ron and I got pretty good at "zig and zag" responses when the "crossfire" started. Due to scheduling, there were some days that we would do these meetings back to back...one in the morning and one in the afternoon, which created a powerful headache by the end of the day. Meanwhile, we still had a company to run.

The outside consultant had predicted that to secure the necessary financing, a two-tier loan would be needed. When I asked what that meant he said, "Two banks provide the funds, with one being the primary lender and the other being the secondary lender with a higher risk position and, thus, charging a higher interest rate." The consultant felt this might be necessary since GPI did not own a lot of tangible assets relative to the anticipated borrowings, and because our financial history was so erratic.

The idea of having to be constantly "hounded" by two groups of bankers instead of one was not something we wanted to do for very long. When I suggested to our consultant that we were going to try and convince one bank to do the whole deal his response was, "good luck."

Most of the presentations were done at our offices in Omaha since each one included a visit to several of our units and a product sampling of our pizza combinations. The presentations were made over a period of about three months before we finally got a "yes" from a bank, which also agreed to do the whole deal...we did not have to use two banks! We were obviously very excited, even though it took another four months to finally close the transaction.

When TPC announced that it was going to sell GPI, the morale of the company was dampened once again due to the cloud of uncertainty that a pending change of ownership creates. After having gone through two ownership changes in two years, the system was justifiably nervous again. It was a real challenge of leadership to keep the people in the company focused so we would not slip back into a sales decline. In the face of the debt we were trying to secure, a sales decline could "kill" Godfather's. Fortunately, that great "turnaround" year had inspired many people to hang in there.

In anticipation of closing the deal and in order to send a message that the completion of the deal was in sight, we planned our second system-wide meeting for September of 1988. The objective of that meeting was to recreate the excitement that we had created at our first system-wide meeting. When we set the date for that meeting four months out, we thought that the closing would have been long since completed based on what the bank had told us. But there was, seemingly, a never-ending stream of details that dragged on and on and on.

When the bank saw our sales trends continue and how committed Ron and I were to GPI, they finally got serious about closing the deal, but their lead attorney would not commit to a closing date. When I explained we had planned a system-wide meeting for September 16th to lift the morale of our people and franchise owners, he seemed unimpressed and mentioned that closing by the 16th (which was about a month away after three months of work already) would interfere with a vacation he had planned. It was at this point that I had to invoke the "get ugly" principle in order to initiate action at a higher level. We were not going to announce to our system on September 16th that "we *almost* own the company." I told this young "whipper-snapper" that we were more concerned about the future of our company than his vacation...nothing personal.

In this case the "get ugly" principle worked and the closing took place in New York on the morning of September 16, 1988! Immediately after the signing of what seemed like thousands of documents, Ron, Gary Batenhorst, and I caught an afternoon flight to Tampa where the all-systems meeting was to begin that night with an opening reception.

When we arrived at the meeting site the reception had already begun and although people knew that we were supposed to close the deal that day, no one knew we had actually gotten it done. We entered the reception where all eyes were on us. We said hellos and shook some hands as we made our way to the front of the room where a microphone was set up.

I walked up to the mike and a total silence descended on the room. I then formally greeted everyone and said, "At approximately 12:30 this afternoon we closed the LBO and we are now the new, heavily in-debt owners of Godfather's Pizza, Inc." After a long and enthusiastic round of applause I simply said, "Let the real celebration party begin!"

The format of the second all-systems meeting in Tampa included two outside speakers. At the first all-systems meeting I was the outside speaker because I was the "new guy."

I invited Don Beveridge to speak because I had heard him at a Burger King national convention, where he made a riveting point that I never forgot—*"you will never again have a competitive advantage on product or price...service is the only advantage."* Even though I

had said this to our people, I also wanted them to hear it from someone else. The national convention where I heard Don make his point
was the same convention where my career at BKC was nearly "hung"
without a trial.

My second guest speaker was Al Reis, the co-author of the book I
found on the airplane in 1986 entitled *Marketing Warfare.* His message about focus was a perfect complement to Don's message on service.

I then closed the meeting, but what could I say that was more
inspiring than the closing speech at that first all systems meeting? You
be the judge:

Godfather's Pizza, Inc.—1988 Convention

*As we come to the end of this 1988 convention, we come to the
beginning of a new passage. We must now salute our past and
celebrate our future. Our 15-year history is now a benchmark
by which to measure our future. We have learned some very
painful lessons which have made us stronger, not weaker.
During the last 15 years, and for some, even as we speak, we
have been down, but never out. Some of you may recall that
my grandfather was a Georgia farmer all his life. One of the
crops he would raise each year was potatoes. Ironically he
would take a wagon load of potatoes into town to sell at the
farmer's market. And he would always get top dollar for a
wagon load of potatoes because he would have separated the
big potatoes from the little potatoes. But he didn't spend hours
and hours of manual labor to separate the potatoes. He would
simply take the roughest roads into town. By the time he got
there all of the little potatoes would have worked their way to
the bottom, while the big potatoes were nicely on the top of the
heap. So regardless of the road you had to endure to be here
today, as part of the Godfather's Pizza system, as a franchisee,*

*an operator, a restaurant manager, a corporate employee, a
supplier, or a distributor, we are all big potatoes.*

*The road has been rough, the Death Valley years, the deep
pan. Moving the corporate office to California and then back
to Omaha. Four presidents of the company in three years.
Massive advertising by our competitors. But there have been a
lot of bright spots along the way...a stronger infrastructure,
improved operations, some marketing successes and some
marketing disappointments, significant growth in our delivery
business, and withstanding another change of ownership. But
this time maintaining management stability. The big potatoes
have survived and despite the roads over which we have traveled and despite everything that has happened to us, we are in
a better condition today as a system than we have been in five
years.*

*And now we set sail for our future. We enter this new pas-
sage from different backgrounds. With different success and
different disappointments. Different experiences and different
perspectives and different expectations. But regardless of
whether you got here on a little ship, a big ship, a losing ship,
a profitable ship, friendship, no ship or the good ship
lollipop...*we are all in the same boat today. *There is room in
this boat for only the big potatoes who believe in the future of
Godfather's as a system. This boat only has room for those that*
believe *we can withstand the evolution of the world around us
and withstand the competitive shots from the "big guys." This
boat only has room for those who truly* believe *the philosophies
of focus, unconditional service, and uncompromising quality.*

*Christopher Columbus believed that the earth was round.
And in 1492 he discovered America. His beliefs changed the
history of America. The early settlers of our country believed
that they wanted freedom from British dominance. They truly
believed that they could defeat the British in war to gain their
independence. And they in fact did, signing the Declaration of*

*Independence in 1776. If the original 13 colonies had not
believed in their freedom and their future we might still have
taxation without representation. And instead of the freedom to
enjoy coffee breaks, at meetings and conventions, we might
have been compelled by British tradition to be having tea
breaks. But the 13 colonies forged ahead as a new nation
based on common beliefs. Most of the breakthrough advances
in medical and biological science have occurred within the
last 100 years. Scientists attribute this in large part to the natu-
ralist, Charles Darwin, who established evolution as a fact,
and showed how it was brought about. According to the
Encyclopedia Britannica, before Charles Darwin's work on
evolution, biology was in a state of chaos. Darwin's belief
changed the course of biological and medical history. Dr.
Jonas Edward Salk believed that polio could be prevented, and
in 1954 completed the development of a polio vaccine that has
virtually eliminated polio in the developed countries of the
world. Martin Luther King Jr., Nobel Peace Prize recipient,
believed that although it would take generations to desegregate
hearts and minds, we could desegregate our social institutions
non-violently. And in 1964 the Civil Rights Act was signed into
law. Ever since the end of World War II, Russia and the United
States had been toying with outer space exploration. To put a
man on the moon. But it wasn't until President John F.
Kennedy declared that the United States would put a man on
the moon by the end of the decade of the 60s...that this became
an achievable, mobilized expectation. Kennedy's belief made it
possible on July 20, 1969 for Neil Armstrong to take "one small
step for man and one giant step for mankind."*

*McDonalds is considered the greatest chain restaurant suc-
cess story in our industry, because of size, consistent growth,
and consistent philosophy. And although the McDonald brothers, Richard and Maurice, pioneered assembly-line hamburg-
ers, it was the genius of Ray Kroc that created a mega-*

corporation based on a simple hamburger concept. But according to John Love in his book, "McDonalds Behind the Arches," Ray Kroc's genius was not product innovation, marketing innovation, or even operational innovation, his driving belief was not centered around food service, table service, counter service, or even window service. Ray Kroc's genius was his uncompromising belief in service. Period. And from the first day he set foot onto that hamburger outlet in San Bernardino, California, in 1954, run by Dick and Mac McDonald, Ray Kroc recognized and maintained uncompromising beliefs in service—a belief around which he motivated, harnessed, and sustained a successful restaurant concept which revolutionized our industry. Although Domino's is one of our major competitors, one can't help but give credit where credit is due. Tom Monahan not only believed in service, but he believed in himself. In the early, early years of Domino's evolution, Tom Monahan was down more than he was up, but never out. And although he looked bankruptcy in the eyes more than once, he believed in his product. He believed in pizza, and more importantly, he believed in himself. Monahan's beliefs revolutionized the pizza restaurant industry.

I'm certain that if you could ask Monahan or Ray Kroc, they would tell you that they didn't do it alone. If you could ask Kennedy or King, they would say they didn't do it alone. Neither Salk, Darwin, nor Columbus could have done it alone. If the original 13 colonies had not pulled together, they would have never become the 13 states of the United States of America. I'm reminded of the words to a song that I learned in grade school that says, "No man is an island, no man stands alone, each man's joy is joy to me, each man's grief is my own. We need one another so I will defend each man as my brother, each man as my friend."

As the Godfather's Pizza system sets sail for the future, the key question is what do you believe? What do you believe

*about life? What do you believe about yourself? What do you
believe about other people? And what do you believe about the
future of Godfather's? I can't answer those questions for you.
But I can certainly tell you what I believe.*

*First, I believe that our Creator put us on this earth to make
a difference—to make a positive impact on the lives of other
people, whether that's in our family, our business, our church,
or our country. If we make a positive contribution, we will
make a positive difference to the people around us. I also
believe that, "Life is just a minute, only 60 seconds in it.
Forced upon me, can't refuse it, didn't seek it, didn't choose it,
but it's up to me to use it. I must suffer if I lose it, give an
account if I abuse it, just a tiny little minute, but eternity is in
it." Secondly, I believe in myself. I grew up in Atlanta, Georgia,
during a time when the schools in the South were totally segregated. And in many instances, the black schools were not as
well-equipped or staffed as the white schools across town.
While I was in high school one of my teachers pointed out that
I had, and was getting, and would probably always have an
inferior education. Fortunately, there was another teacher who
I still remember that told me and others in my class, that
although our education may have been inferior in some
respects, we were not inferior. He also told us we could be
whatever we wanted to be in life, if we believed in ourselves
and were willing to work a little harder to get there.*

*My parents were from very humble beginnings, with a less
than modest life-style. In other words, we were technically poor
during my early childhood, but my brother and I didn't know
it. We did not know we were poor because we had a roof over
our heads, and food to eat and parents, fortunately, who
cared about us, and taught us basic values, such as respect,
integrity, and consideration for other people. They also sent us
both to college, with my mother working domestically and my
father working three jobs simultaneously as a chauffeur, a*

*barber, and a night janitor. Ironically, this night janitor job
was with the Atlanta Refrigerated Dough Plant for the
Pillsbury Company in the late 50s. I believe in myself, because
someone else made a difference in my life.*

*My belief in myself was inspired not only by my parents,
and that one teacher who fought inferior surroundings with
superior encouragement. I was also inspired by Dr. Benjamin
E. Mays, the late President Emeritus of Morehouse College
where I attended college, who said,* "Failure isn't not reaching
your goal, failure is not reaching high enough." *But since
human nature is the way it is, I was also inspired in other
ways. A former boss told me prior to entering Purdue
University for graduate school that I probably would not finish
the master's degree program because I probably would not be
able to maintain the required 3.0 average. He had concluded
this based on his assessment of the quality of my educational
background, rather than on the quality of the man. As a result
of his words of* "motivation," *I finished the master's degree program with a 3.4 grade point average. A former Burger King
executive told me that I would not make it in Burger King
because they intended to* "put me through the wringer" *while I
was learning operations after leaving a secure Pillsbury VP
position. I finished the 18-month program in 9 months and
was assigned to the Philadelphia region as Vice President and
General Manager. I must have been doing something right,
because 3 and a half years later I was asked to become the
President of Godfather's Pizza. When I came to Godfather's,
some of my then Pillsbury and BK colleagues did not believe
we would be here today, talking about our future. Some of our
industry associates did not believe that Godfather's Pizza had
any* "Big Potatoes." *When I came to Godfather's 2 and a half
years ago, I came without a golden parachute. And I came
committed to prove the skeptics WRONG! AND WE DID!!*

In February 1988, I was officially informed that

*Godfather's Pizza was going to be sold because it did not fit
Pillsbury's strategic future. This was obviously an emotional
blow to me and my management team because we were
excited about the progress we were making, and the progress
and support of you, our franchisees. Since we believed in what
we had been doing, we decided to buy the company.
Obviously, not everyone believed we would be able to complete
the deal because of the hurdles and the hoops we would have
to overcome. It was too highly leveraged, the historical financials were discouraging, and the history of the company was
no bed of roses. But we believed we could do it and we did.*

*My belief in myself is inspired every time someone says,
"Can't, maybe, I doubt it, or yeah…but," because as Henry
Ford said, "Whether you believe you can, or you believe you
can't, in either case, you're right." I believe in myself because I
do not believe in those small, thornless, motionless, spineless,
parasitic creatures called, "yeah, buts."*

*Thirdly, I believe in other people, other people who are win-
ners. Winners are the right people, with the right stuff, in the
right game, with the right coach. I stood before you 2 and a
half years ago and first declared, "Them that's going…get on
the wagon, Them that ain't… get out of the way." I was later
informed that some of our constituencies did not believe we
were serious about yanking victory from the jaws of defeat. All
of you are here today because you were and still are able to
dream and commit. I believe in other people who are winners
even though it makes me vulnerable to disappointments and
sets me up for letdowns. But believing in other people who are
winners is a necessary condition for success.*

*What do you believe? I can't answer that for you. I know
that Ron Gartland believes in Godfather's Pizza. I know that
our management group believes in Godfather's Pizza. I also
know that many of you believe in Godfather's Pizza and in us.
We believe in the future of Godfather's, we believe in ourselves,*

A Leader Must . . .

Remove Barriers
Lead
Inspire

and we believe in you! It doesn't matter how you got here today, it doesn't matter. Whether you are a small operator or a large operator... it does not matter. What we may have dis-agreed on in the past... it doesn't matter. Whether we are fran-chisee or franchisor, we are all in the same boat. And since we're in the same boat, one does not have to be a rocket scien-tist to figure out that if we work in the same direction Godfather's Pizza will become a great ship in that great big sea of restaurants. But only if there are no leaks. And as Ben Franklin said, "A small leak will sink a great ship."

We will be successful with a few good people who have the inner-vision to dream. We will be successful with a few good people who have the tenacity to commit. We will be successful with a few "big potatoes" with the desire to compete and make things happen. "There is no joy in easy sailing, when the skies are clear and blue. Nor is there joy in merely doing things that anyone can do. But there is some satisfaction that is mighty sweet to take, when you reach a destination along this journey you thought you'd never make."

We have reached an unexpected destination, but we believe in Godfather's!

The Godfather's story in the 28 months since I had been its president was not only industry news, it was also news. In a published textbook case study of Godfather's by the M.I.T. Sloan School of Management, the author made a most flattering comment: "In the twenty-eight months since he (Cain) had joined Godfather's Pizza, Cain had achieved what more than one industry observer had characterized as a miracle." I think that the word "miracle" is a bit strong, and leaders don't achieve the unexpected alone. I am deeply grateful to all of the people who made those first 28 months at Godfather's an adventure, but especially to Ronald B. Gartlan and Gary R. Batenhorst.

Two weeks after the second all-systems meeting, I was attending a conference in Washington, D.C. where I was asked to give a speech on how we were able to put the LBO together. On the morning after my speech, I was headed for the general session when an acquaintance said, "What do you think about the Pillsbury deal?" I said, "You mean the deal we made to buy GPI?" He said, "No. The tender offer by Grand Metropolitan to buy Pillsbury." I said, "You *are* kidding!" He then told me the story was in the *Wall Street Journal.*

I immediately turned around and went back to my room to call Ron, my partner, and asked him, "What is happening at Pillsbury!?" Ron said he only knew what was in the *Wall Street Journal.*

More importantly, Ron and I speculated about what might have happened if we had not closed our deal when we did. We both concluded that we would *not* have been able to structure the deal we did with the new owners, because according to the WSJ it was a "hostile" takeover attempt.

When I was forced to "get ugly" with the bank's attorneys to make certain we had the LBO done by the time of our September 16, 1988 all-systems meeting, I did not have the slightest idea that this "get ugly" was a two-for-one...*one* for our all-systems meeting and *one* for the deal itself.

The old saying that "timing is everything" is not only true, it is twice as true. However, I didn't call it luck as some people would say, I simply said...THANK YOU GOD!

It's Working

Ron and I felt prepared for the challenge of putting nearly everything we owned on the line and betting our futures on our belief in the Godfather's concept, but most importantly, betting our futures on our belief in ourselves.

We were also prepared in another way...complementary strengths and experiences. Ron had been a very successful partner in one of the major public accounting firms prior to joining GPI in 1982, and then had been hired by GPI to handle the original public offering of GPI. Ron was also involved with the sale of the company to Diversifoods in 1983, the sale of the company to TPC in 1985, and then our purchase of the company in 1988. He was and is without question, imminently prepared for the financial challenges of creating and maintaining a successful company.

During our negotiations with TPC and the bank, I saw another major strength in Ron as a businessman. He is one of the most effective and tenacious negotiators I have ever worked with, and his integrity is beyond reproach. On many occasions I have told him, "I'm glad you're on my side."

My strengths have most often been described by those I have worked with over the years as highly self motivated, entrepreneurial, focused, able to cut to the heart of an issue, not afraid to make a decision and able to inspire..."three plus three." It has also been said that I am a pretty decent public speaker.

In terms of our values about life and family, Ron and I are as alike as two people can get. In terms of our personalities, we are as opposite as you can get. I am considered an extrovert and Ron more of an introvert. I have never found a podium that I did not like, and Ron has never found one that he did like. He hates to give speeches to groups unless he absolutely has to and then he does a great job. I, on the other hand, am not reluctant to give a speech...it's a dirty job but someone has to do it. Ron is usually more moderate in his day-to-day demeanor, whereas I am usually more upbeat. In fact, someone has to work real hard to "tick me off" or put me in a bad mood, and if they do, it only happens once.

Having complementary skills, abilities, experiences, and even personalities between business partners is something one can hope for but rarely find. Ron and I are one of those rare occasions. Even more rare is that on top of it all, we are also friends.

Eight years after closing the LBO, GPI has *never* been out of compliance with the bank on any of its financial requirements. This has been our number one priority, since default in any way would give the bank all the leverage in defining how the default could be cured. We did not like some of the easy actions the bank *could* demand in order to cure the default, such as sell off one of our most profitable company markets, which they had hinted at several times during the approval process.

When the "real celebration party" began, the real work also began. The bank's long-term interest was and is to recoup their investment plus as much interest and fees as legally possible, not whether GPI will be around long term. I do not mean to suggest that our bank or all bankers are like that old joke about a banker being someone who offers you an umbrella when the sun is shining but wants it back when it is raining...it just seems that way. Bankers are just tenacious about protecting their investments, as all good businesspeople are.

During the first two years of our debt arrangement there were quarterly reviews with the bank to review how we were doing, but, more importantly, how well we would continue to be able to comply with all covenants. Things went so well that soon quarterly reviews became every six months, then annually with a monthly written recap of our financial condition.

About four years after we closed our deal, we were able to buy back the portion of our deal financed by Pillsbury. Although it was approximately 20 percent of the total transaction, we took great pride in being able to achieve this, using cash from the opportunistic sale of an asset. This transaction got TPC totally out of the picture and enhanced our cash flow.

The next milestone occurred when we were able to restructure our loan and buy back some outstanding "warrants" held by the bank. The warrants were basically a right of the bank to invoke the purchase of a minority share of the company if it proved in their best interest. At the same time we bought the warrants back and eliminated another outside partner, we were financially strong enough to establish a line of credit for new company store development. The implication of this extended beyond just financial because it was a tremendous boost to morale that we could now begin to grow again with new restaurant units.

We have been able to maintain our basic benefits and health insurance plans, even though President Clinton tried to make it unaffordable. We have also been able to establish an employee 401(k) plan where we have made voluntary company contributions to the plan to benefit all participants at the end of particularly good performance years.

We have increased the number of company units from about 150 in 1988 to over 200 in 1996, which represents 38 percent of the total units in the system. Most of the franchise owners that seriously "got on the wagon" with us are also doing well.

During the last eight years we have never shown a loss and most importantly, *we have never defaulted on any of our covenants with the bank.*

Maintaining GPI as a healthy business continues to be a challenge because of changing competitive conditions, changing economic conditions, and the continued threat to free enterprise by the "ations" (legislation, taxation, and regulation). But it is a challenge that we continue to enjoy because as Spirella wrote, "There is no joy in easy sailing."

Eight years and counting...its working pretty well!

The LBO presented many leadership challenges beyond just managing the business. We could no longer fall back on Pillsbury if cash flow became strained, or obtain capital for new development at their more favorable cost of capital. We no longer had access to the Pillsbury reservoir of corporate expertise just waiting to lend their help, nor the ability to obtain relief from not showing a profit due to explainable but unexpected events. As owners of the company, we had to maintain its viability to generate our own paychecks as well as the paychecks of over 10,000 other people in the GPI system. These are the sobering realities of ownership and that old saying..."the buck stops here."

CHAPTER 4

ATTACK OF THE HERMANATOR... THE RESTAURANT INDUSTRY "B.I.T.E.s" BACK

"We hold these truths to be self-evident, that all Men are created equal, that they are endowed by their Creator with certain unalienable Rights, that among these are Life, Liberty, and the Pursuit of Happiness..."

The Declaration of Independence
Action of Second Continental Congress
July 4, 1776

The Question

"On behalf of all of those business owners that are in a situation similar to mine, my question is, quite simply, if I'm forced to do this, what will I tell those people whose jobs I will have to eliminate?"

It started with a phone call from Loretta Carroll, news anchor for KMTV in Omaha, on April 6, 1994. I just happened to be in my office that morning—a rare occurrence since in recent weeks I had been out of town a great deal, giving speeches against the proposed Clinton Health Care Plan. As Vice President of the National Restaurant Association (NRA), I was part of a nationwide initiative to help raise awareness that the Clinton plan, although well intended, was an economic and social disaster.

Loretta called to ask my opinion on a comment President Clinton had made the evening before at a town hall meeting in South Carolina. He had stated, in essence, that the cost of his health care plan for service businesses like restaurants would only be about two and one-half percent of the cost of doing business, and that he did not understand why the restaurant industry's opposition was so intense.

Loretta asked me what I thought of that comment, and I responded that it was ludicrous! My staff and I had been through the calculations many times, and we continued to find that for many restaurant businesses, the president's calculations were off—way off. Loretta then asked if she could quote me on this and I said yes, and she did so on the 10 p.m. news that night.

Before we ended our conversation, Loretta also asked if I would attend the president's town hall meeting the next night. Mr. Clinton was to be in Kansas City but he would be taking questions "live" from audiences in Omaha, Nebraska, Tulsa, Oklahoma, and Topeka, Kansas—all via communications hook-ups. I said, "I will be happy to." Loretta also asked if I would be prepared to ask the president a question if I got the chance. Again, I answered affirmatively. Having interviewed me on previous occasions and knowing how passionate I can be on an issue which I believe in, Loretta advised me to "be respectful." "Of course I will," I responded.

April 7, 1994 started out as a typical business day for me. I spent some time that morning in the office before catching a plane to western Nebraska where I was scheduled to give a speech at Nebraska's Hastings College. After that, I had to hustle back onto an airplane and return to Omaha in order to be at the studio in time for the town hall meeting.

When I arrived at KMTV's west Omaha studio around 6:30 p.m., station officials were checking names off an invitation list. They were also asking each of us to write out the questions we would ask the president if given the opportunity. To this day, I cannot remember what question I wrote at check-in, but I doubt that it had anything to do with the question I actually asked during my "chat" with the president.

Looking around the room, it appeared as if I were one of about 100 people in the audience, some of whom I recognized from various community and business functions during my eight years in Omaha. One person I did not recognize was sitting in front of me. I would later learn he was a reporter for the *Omaha World Herald* who would ask me a few follow-up questions, which he used in his story the following day.

When the telecast began, the president took his first question from an audience member in Kansas City. He eventually proceeded, in a rotational manner, to audiences in the other participating cities. I was not asked to speak during the first rotation to Omaha, and quite frankly, I was pleased because it gave me a chance to get a feel for the program's format, along with a better appreciation of the president's style and manner in this sort of setting. But more importantly, I had an opportunity to think more about that one question I might have an opportunity to ask.

By the end of the first round of questions, I was a little disappointed with what I had been hearing. I felt the questions had, for the most part, been a little too "touchy-feely," platitudinous, generally emotional, and not factual. I realized later that many other people felt the same way—especially the media people covering this event. No one seemed to be speaking to the hard core facts of the president's plan. I realized then that if given the opportunity, I had to address something concrete about the president's plan, rather than ask another "la la land" question that just made some people feel good. This was simply too important an issue to waste lobbying another "softball" question.

As the second rotation to Omaha neared, Ms. Carroll, who was also the local studio moderator, approached me and said, "Herman—you can ask your question next." I thought I detected in her tone of voice an annoyance that the questions weren't generating much excitement. Unknowingly, that was all about to change.

I was ready when the Kansas City moderator said, "Okay, we will now take another question from Omaha."

"Mr. President," Loretta said, "Tuesday in North Carolina we talked about the cost of health care reform for service industries, specifically restaurants. Here with me now is Herman Cain, the CEO of Godfather's Pizza. He has some concerns about that."

I have to admit this was one of the few times in my life that I really felt a little nervous. It was not nervousness because of Bill Clinton, or because I was on a television broadcast—I had been on TV many times before. No, it was nervousness because of my respect for the office of President of the United States of America, the "position" of the greatest nation on the face of the earth.

Just before I stood up, and still not knowing exactly what I would say, I prayed my favorite prayer: "Not my will O Lord, but thy will be done." I began to speak.

"Mister President, thank you very much for this opportunity and I would first like to commend you on making health care a national priority."

He nodded politely.

"In your State of the Union speech, you indicated that nine out of ten Americans currently have health care insurance, primarily

through their employers. And tonight you indicated that out of those people who do not have insurance, eight out of ten of them work for someone. And your plan would force employers to pay this insurance for those people that they currently do not cover. I would contend that employers who do not cover employees, do not for one simple reason and it relates to cost."

Next I explained I had calculated what his program would cost Godfather's Pizza, Inc., and that I had also spoken with hundreds of other business people about his program's impact on their operations. *"The cost of your plan is simply a cost that will cause us to eliminate jobs,"* I explained. *"In going through my own calculations, the number of jobs that we would have to eliminate to try to absorb this cost is a lot greater than I ever anticipated. Your averages about the impact on smaller businesses—those are all well intended—but all of the averages represent a wide spectrum in terms of the businesses impacted."*

Now I came to the gist of the matter, and what would eventually become a soundbite repeated on news broadcasts across the country during the next 24 hours. *"On behalf of all of those business owners that are in a situation similar to mine, my question is, quite simply, if I'm forced to do this, what will I tell those people whose jobs I will have to eliminate?"*

At this point, I paused to allow the president to respond, and to catch my breath because I felt as if I had not taken a breath at all up until that point. The following is a transcript taken from the broadcast from this point in the exchange:

The Non-Answer

President Clinton:

"Let's talk a minute about what you would have to do. Are any of your employees insured now?"

Herman Cain:

"Yes Sir. Approximately one-third of my employees are insured now."

President Clinton:

And of the third that are insured now, what percent of payroll does their insurance cost?

Herman Cain:

"My insurance costs at the present time run approximately two and one-half percent of payroll."

President Clinton:

"And what do you provide them with? They share the cost fifty-fifty or something like that?"

Herman Cain:

"Seventy-five percent is paid for by my company and twenty-five percent is paid for by the employee. Now, two-thirds of my employees are part-time or short-term workers that fall into the class you identified earlier."

President Clinton:

"Okay. If they are part-time or short-time workers, they wouldn't add all that much. You wouldn't have to pay the whole seven point nine percent for them because they don't work all the time. Let me ask you this. On the average, food service business payroll is about one-third the total cost of doing business. Is that about what it is?"

Herman Cain:

"That's an adequate estimation, yes sir."

President Clinton:

"So suppose you have part-time workers and some wouldn't have to be covered. So you wouldn't go from two and one-half percent of payroll to seven point nine percent. You might go to something like six percent. If you had six percent of payroll...let's just say six and one-half percent, that's a good, even number. You had four percent of payroll—and that's one-third of your total cost. So you would add about one and a half percent to the total cost of doing business. Would that really cause you to lay a lot of people off? If all your competitors have to do it, too? Only if people stopped eating out. If all your competitors had to do it and your cost of doing business went up one and a half percent...wouldn't that leave you in the same position you are in now? Why wouldn't they all be in the same position? And why wouldn't you all be able to raise the price of pizza two percent? I'm a satisfied customer. I'd keep buying from you.

The Kansas City audience found this last statement humorous, and there was laughter. It is interesting that not one person in the Omaha studio audience laughed.

"This is a very important question because a huge number of Americans are involved in the food industry. Forty percent of the American food dollar is spent eating out now—forty percent—so this is not an idle question. This man is asking a very important question in terms of employment.

"What if all your competitors were just like you? Wouldn't you be able to do it then?"

Instead of first answering my question, the president proceeded to try and convince me and the audience that the impact of his plan on my business (and therefore, on other restaurants and small businesses) would be minimal. In fact, it was obvious after reviewing the transcript of our conversation that he was attempting to lead me to the two and one-half percent number he had used in North Carolina two nights before. In addition, his "barrage" of questions and totally confusing arithmetic appeared more for the purpose of positioning than to genuinely seek information.

When he started down this path of dialogue, I thought, "I do not believe he is going to try and prove to me and the world that his two and one-half percent number is right."

Just the previous day, I had asked the staff of the National Restaurant Association to try and determine how the president had arrived at that number he used in North Carolina. After some checking, no one could determine with certainty how he came up with two and one-half percent. Bill Fisher, Executive Vice President of our association, speculated that the president (or his staff) simply multiplied (a) the maximum percent of payroll (7.9 percent) a company would have to pay under the Clinton plan, times (b) the average labor as a percent of sales (30 percent) in the restaurant industry, which equals 2.7 percent (rounded). This is exactly the arithmetic the president used during our four-minute "chat" on national TV.

The problem was, and continues to be, that his arithmetic was, and is, mathematically incorrect! *Seven point nine percent of a cost (labor dollars) is a 7.9 percent increase. Seven point nine percent of a percent cost (30 percent) is not a cost increase...it's just bad arith-metic.*

Then the president asked, "Why wouldn't you all (competitors) be able to raise the price of pizza two percent?" Once again, the president had tried to make the impact of his plan on the restaurant industry seem minimal—not only by using an incorrect calculation, but by rounding down from 2.7 percent to 2 percent .

First of all, the cost increase in this case is 7.9 percent, not 2 percent or 2.4 percent, and secondly, it would be illegal (price fixing) for all competitors to raise their prices the same, even if the government made us do it. Plus, I believe "all us competitors" would lose business if such a plan were instituted because the consumer would eventually buy less of something when they had less money to spend. Obviously, this is an unfamiliar concept to many politicians. Furthermore, the smaller competitors would lose the most. Even if the president's proposal were possible, to pass along a 7.9 percent cost increase to our customers in the form of a price increase would require about a 16 percent price increase on the products my company sells. The difference is that a dollar on the "top line" of a profit and loss statement does not produce a dollar on the "bottom line." Therefore, to capture a 7.9 percent cost increase off the "bottom line," businesses have to generate a much larger percentage on the "top line."

Herman Cain:

"Okay. First of all, Mr. President, with all due respect, your calculation on what the impact would do, quite honestly, is incorrect.

Let's take, for example, the fact that after I went through my calculations, your calculations and your example of the six percent or the seven point nine—and in my case it works out to seven point nine percent. Now, let's suppose that thirty percent of my costs are labor costs. Seven point nine times that would be the two and one-half percent that you're referring to. The problem with that calculation, sir, is the fact that most of those thirty percent of the people currently have zero. So when I calculate in the fact that I have to go from no coverage on these employees to full coverage at the seven point nine percent rate, it actually works out to be approximately sixteen percent.

"Now your other point about having to pass it on to my customers. In the competitive market place, it simply doesn't work that way because the larger competitors have more staying power before they go bankrupt than a smaller competitor. They have more staff that they can simply do without until the market place re-establishes itself. So what I am saying and suggesting is that the assumptions about the impact on a business like mine are simply not correct because we are very labor-intensive. We have a large number of part-time and short-term employees that we do not cover for one simple reason—we can't afford it.

My bottom line net profit for the last two years was less than one and a half percent of my top line sales. When we calculate the cost just for my company under your plan, it equates to three times what my bottom line profitability is. So what is one of the biggest misconceptions, sir, is the fact that a company like mine only makes between one and three percent of top line sales. And because we have a large population of employees that we would like to cover but simply the dynamics of our business would not allow us to do that under your proposed plan."

The president then responded, *"Let me ask you a favor. Would you send to me, personally, your calculations because I know we've got to go on to other questions. But let me remind you, if it added four and a half percent to the cost of doing business—and his labor costs were only one-third of his total costs, then all you have to do is multiply it by three. It would have to be thirteen and one-half percent of payroll and maximum is seven point nine. So we can't get there. So we'll work on it."*

This closing statement was based, again, on incorrect math. It made absolutely no sense. When the camera's red light went off, the telecast switched back to Kansas City. I sat down in my seat and the Omaha studio audience gave me a round of enthusiastic applause. At that moment I really did not know why.

I did send the president my calculations (see the insert), in a letter which appeared in the *Wall Street Journal,* the *Omaha World Herald,* and several other newspapers (see Exhibit 4–1). And the response I received from the head of the Small Business

Exhibit 4-1 *Transcript of Herman Cain's letter to the President from the* Wall Street Journal*

I Can't Afford Your Health Plan, Mr. Clinton

Dear Mr. President:

During your April 7, 1994 town hall telecast from Kansas City, you asked me to send you my calculations of the impact on our business of your health care proposal. I am happy to do so in this letter.

As a reminder, the Godfather's Pizza system has 525 restaurants with over 10,000 employees. Two-thirds of these restaurants are owned and operated by franchisees of our company, whose operating financials are almost identical to our corporate-owned operations of 141 restaurants. Therefore, in order to be as specific as possible in our calculations, I will focus on just our corporate-owned operations with 3,418 employees.

Under your proposed health care plan, the cost to cover all 3,418 employees would be nearly $2.2 million annually. This amount of $2.2 million is a $1.7 million increase in our insurance, which is approximately 3½ times our prior-year insurance cost. Last year we paid $540,000 in insurance premiums to cover an 80% employer portion for all participating full-time employees.

You mentioned during the telecast that restaurants with approximately 30% labor need only increase prices 2.5%. This price increase appears to be arrived at by taking 7.9% times 30%. Quite frankly, we cannot just look at a percent of a percent but instead we must look at the actual dollars involved. A $1.7 million cost increase would directly decrease "bottom line" profit. In order to produce the same "bottom line" as we are generating today, a 16%-20% increase in "top line" sales would be required due to variable costs such as labor, food costs, operating expenses, marketing, and taxes. Thus, it is incorrect to assume we can just add $1.7 million to the "top line" and expect it to flow directly to the "bottom line."

As a system of small businesses, we are concerned about the impact of any price increase for the following reasons:

1. Large price increases will drive customers away. Over 50% of our customers use coupons with their pizza purchases because they are very price conscious. In fact, 25% of all restaurant customers use a discount coupon with their purchase. (Source: NPD/CREST)

2. Since it is likely that many of our suppliers of ingredients and materials will also experience increases in costs due to a mandate, they will likely pass some or all of those costs on to us and, thus, it becomes an inflationary *"snowball."*

3. Although consumers are spending more of their food dollar eating out, it is due to competitive forces which tend to hold prices down. This is evidenced by the cost of eating out rising slower than the cost of eating at home (Source: Consumer Price Index, Bureau of Labor Statistics). I believe price increases "by all competitors" in our industry would change this trend.

To summarize, Godfather's Pizza, Inc. employs a large percent (67%) of younger, inexperienced, and minimum-educated workers with a very high turnover rate of over 100% annually. This is typical of all quick service restaurants, which account for 47% of all eating place sales. I wish we could cover this group of workers, but the incremental cost under your plan causes a significant negative impact on our "bottom line" which cannot be easily rectified. We would then be put in a position to eliminate jobs which would impact productivity and ultimately profitability, or to increase prices to the point of being at a competitive disadvantage.

Mr. President, I believe your objective of coverage for everyone can be achieved without a mandate, using an alternate approach *to health care reform . . . but this is what the debate is all about. I will not impose on the courtesy you have extended to me to personally review my calculations, but I will be more than happy to share some ideas with you personally on alternate approaches which are more business friendly and public friendly.*

Thank you for your very valuable time and attention; I look forward to your response.

> *Most respectfully,*
> *Herman Cain*

Administration, Erskine Bowles, did not challenge my calculations, logic, or rationale. Instead, his response attempted to rationalize how much better off society, in general, would be under the president's plan, regardless of its impact on business or the economy.

That letter was the last I heard from the president or his administration.

The Morning After

I will never forget April 8, 1994, the day following the town hall meeting telecast.

My wife, Gloria, was watching "Good Morning America" when she called out, "Herman, you're on TV!" (I was getting dressed, preparing to go to my office and planning to go about my day...as usual).

I came out to see what was the big deal. There I was—featured in the top of the hour news on "Good Morning America."

Out of curiosity, one of us (I don't remember which one) switched the channel to one of the other network morning shows...and there I was again! We eventually switched to CNN ("Around the World in 30 Minutes") and there I was...again!

I was absolutely shocked that my confrontation had generated such interest with the network news media. Each of the TV news reports highlighted either my question, *"If you force me to do this (the health care plan), what will I tell all those people whose jobs I will have to eliminate?,"* or my response to his calculations, *"Mr. President, with all due respect, your calculations are incorrect"*...or they featured both!

I finally finished getting dressed and left for my office. As usual, I turned on my car radio to catch a few minutes of radio news on the way to work and there "he" was again...the "pizza man," as some reporters referred to the person who challenged the president in his town hall meeting. I was beginning to get the "Twilight Zone" feeling that this was a dream.

When I arrived at my office building around 8:30 a.m. and stepped off the elevator, I said my usual "good morning" to Eva, our corporate receptionist at the time. But instead of her usual cheerful, "good morning" response, the first words out of her mouth were, "The phones are ringing off the hook...I can hardly keep up with the calls coming in." I said, "Calls about what?" Eva said (almost shouting). "Last night, when you talked to the president. People are calling to congratulate you on telling it like it is and for saying what they also felt about the Clinton plan. Calls are coming from all over the country!" Eva was excited. I really was starting to get that "Twilight Zone" feeling.

When I finally got to my office and greeted my executive assistant, Jan, she at least said, "good morning" first. Then she added, "You were great last night...the fax machine is going crazy!" I said, "What's wrong with the fax machine?" Jan responded, "We can't load paper in that sucker fast enough because of all the letters and notes people are sending you about last night!"

Ninety-eight percent of the people who called or wrote or sent faxes were supportive of my position and comments to the president. Those that disagreed simply tried to ignore me, except for one lady who called and talked to Jan because I was on the phone *all day*. This particular lady bent Jan's ear for about 20 minutes, telling her how much she did not like what I said, and did not like my position against the Clinton health care proposal, and did not like the fact that I disagreed with the president. After going on and on, she finally told Jan to tell me that she was "never going to go to Domino's Pizza again!" Jan told her that was a good idea and thanked her for calling.

Faxes were coming from many people who had called the company and figured they would not be able to talk with me in person because of the influx of calls...and they were right.

Over the next several weeks the mail into the corporate office more than doubled each day as people wrote to share their feelings about my dialogue with the president and their opinions about Clinton's health care proposal.

One of the first calls I remember taking the "morning after" was from Jeff Prince at the National Restaurant Association. His first words were, "You are everywhere...all the TV stations, all of the Washington papers...and we are getting dozens of calls for follow-up interviews."

I then got Elaine Graham and Patty Stinger of the NRA on the phone, and they were ecstatic. For months the three of us had been traveling to various states, trying to generate awareness about the *real* impact of the Clinton health care plan—on our industry in particular, and on business in general. Now it was the "topic du jour." Heightened public and business awareness against the Clinton plan had just moved to a new level. Larry Neal of Senator Phil Gramm's staff said in a September 19, 1994 *Newsweek* interview, "...Cain was the lightning rod." By the end of "the morning after" I had come to realize what the Omaha audience had seen and felt the "night before."

The Aftermath

In May of 1994, following the April town hall meeting, I was installed as President of the NRA. This had nothing to do with my instant notoriety but everything to do with NRA by-laws, which provide for leadership succession within the organization, and everything to do with how fellow NRA board members viewed me as a "D, E, & F" kind of guy. Before becoming president, an individual must first have demonstrated leadership skills on various committee assignments, and served as treasurer and vice president. I make this point because at least one Clinton administration official remarked that my attendance at the town hall meeting was a "plant" since I just happened to be president-elect of the NRA. This was not true. When Loretta Carroll, the Omaha broadcaster, called me to ask if I would participate, she was doing so on the basis of my reputation as an Omaha resident and businessman. I do not believe she was even aware of my role in the NRA at that point.

As the newly installed president of the NRA, one of my objectives was to continue our crusade against the Clinton health care plan. Most of my business colleagues and I did not, and could not, support such a flawed approach to this vital issue. Momentum was clearly on our side and before long it was rippling all the way up to Congress. This momentum was crucial to our efforts to *influence* more people to speak out based on facts. Even though members of Congress would determine the fate of the proposed plan, each vote would be influenced by their respective constituencies. Our challenge was to influence their constituencies.

As the 75th president of the NRA in its 75-year history, and having been a member of the board for six years, there were two initiatives that I believed the association needed to focus on in order to be more effective in its fight against the 'ATIONS...legislation, regulation, and taxation. The ton of regulations, taxes, and fees required at the federal, state, and local level is already mind-boggling (Exhibit 4-2), and our elected "leaders" keep passing more and more requirements to try and feed that insatiable appetite for more revenue to feed an out-of-control federal spending habit. Although the NRA has fought hard over the years to counter unfair and unnecessary requirements, it is a difficult ongoing battle because of the complexity of the bureaucracy today. The proposed Clinton Health Care Plan (if passed) would have created even more complexity (barriers) and would have been a

Exhibit 4-2 *Regulations and Restaurants from A to Z*

There's a lot more to running a restaurant than serving good food. People in the restaurant business face a ton of regulations, fees, and permit requirements governing everything from food safety to tip reporting. Here's a partial list of the federal, state, and local rules covering restaurants. (In parentheses is the federal agency that enforces these rules.)

Federal

940 Form (Employer's Annual FUTA Tax Return) (IRS)
941 Form (Employer's Quarterly Federal Tax Return) (IRS)
Accessibility to disabled customers (DOJ)
Advanced payment of Earned Income Credit (IRS)
Age discrimination (EEOC)
Alcohol excise taxes (IRS)
Annual occupational tax for alcohol-sellers (BATF)
Bloodborne pathogen program for employees who give first-aid (OSHA)
Citizenship-status discrimination (DOJ)
Carpools for employers in high-pollution areas (EPA)
Continued health benefits for former employees (IRS)
Cooking emissions in high-pollution areas (EPA)
Copyright law and restaurant music (DOJ)

(continues)

Exhibit 4-2 *Regulations and Restaurants from A to Z (continued)*

EEO-1 Form (EEOC)
Egg refrigeration standards (USDA)
Exempt managers (DOL)
Fair Labor Standards Act (DOL)
Family and Medical Leave Act (DOL)
Federal income taxes (IRS)
Federal income tax withholding for employees (IRS)
FICA payroll taxes (IRS)
FICA payroll taxes on tips (IRS)
FUTA payroll taxes (IRS)
Gaming — cash transaction report (IRS)
Grease-trap waste disposal (EPA)
Hazard Communication Standard (OSHA)
Health claims and restaurant foods (FDA)
Health benefit plans and the Americans with Disabilities Act (EEOC)
I-9 Form (Employment Eligibility Verification Form) (INS)
Immigration Reform and Control Act of 1986 (INS)
Independent contractors, reporting of payments to (IRS)
Job application forms, permissible questions (EEOC)
Lockout/tagout requirements (OSHA)
Magnetic media reporting of Forms W-2, 8027 (IRS, SSA)
Material Safety Data Sheets (OSHA)
Meal credit (DOL)
Minimum wage (DOL)
National Labor Relations Act (NLRB)
National origin discrimination (EEOC)
Notice to employees of eligibility for Earned Income Credit (IRS)
Nutrient-content claims and restaurant foods (FDA)
Overtime pay rules (DOL)
Payroll-tax deposits (IRS)
Personal protective equipment (OSHA)
Polygraph ban (DOL)
Poster: Equal employment opportunity (EEOC)
Poster: Polygraph (DOL)
Poster: Minimum wage (DOL)
Poster: Family and medical leave (DOL)
Poster: OSHA (OSHA)
Race discrimination (EEOC)
Reasonable accommodation for workers with disabilities (EEOC)
Refrigeration equipment and CFC phase-out (EPA)
Religious discrimination (EEOC)
Restaurant closings, 60 day advance notice (DOL)
SS-4 Form (Employer ID Number) (IRS)
Sex discrimination (EEOC)
Teen labor: Hours restrictions for workers under 16 (DOL)
Teen labor: Occupational restrictions for workers under 18 (DOL)
Tip credit (DOL)
Tip reporting and IRS Form 8027 (IRS)
Tip allocation (IRS)
Tip-income audits (IRS)

(continues)

Exhibit 4-2 *Regulations and Restaurants from A to Z (continued)*

Tip pools (DOL)
Uniforms: Deposits, costs, maintenance (DOL)
Union contracts (NLRB)
Veterans' employment rights (DOL)
W-2 Form (Wage and Tax Statement) (IRS, SSA)
W-3 Form (Transmittal of Income and Tax Statements) (IRS)
W-4 Form (Employee's Withholding Allowance Certificate) (IRS)
W-5 Form (Earned Income Credit Advance Payment Certificate) (IRS)

Nebraska

Alcohol Beverage Tax
Beverage Container Tax
Business Licensing Fees
Child Labor Laws
Child Labor Work Permits
Container Tax
Corporation Annual Report Fee
Corporation Excise Tax
Corporate Organization and Qualification Fees
Entertainment License/Fee/Tax
Fire Code Compliance
Fire Monitoring Fee
Happy Hour Law
Hour Restrictions for Employees under 16
Hour Restrictions for Employees 16 & 17 years old
Ice Cream Permit/Fee
Liability Laws
Liquor License/Tax
Meals Tax
Milk Permit/Fee
Minimum Wage Laws
Occupational Restrictions for Minors
Payment of Wage Laws
Personal Income Tax
Poster Requirements
Property Tax
Record Keeping Requirements/Wage Reporting
Restaurant License/Fee
Room Occupancy Tax
Sales and Use Tax
Sanitation/Food Preparation Regulations
Sunday Liquor License/Fee
Termination Payment Law
Tip Credit Law
Unemployment Insurance and Unemployment Tax
Wage Deduction Laws and Wage Exemption Regulations
Workers' Compensation Insurance
Zoning Laws

"knock-out blow" for thousands of businesses. My industry would have been hit especially hard since we are very labor-intensive.

My first initiative was to highlight the need for us to speak as *one voice*. Although some legislative proposals impacted some industry segments differently, the proposed health care plan would have impacted most of us the same...badly. Seasoned politicians knew how to maximize the old adage of "keep 'em divided and do what is politically advantageous." From the day I was installed as president, the one voice message of my presidency was everywhere...in all my speeches to the boards of the 44 state restaurant associations I visited, in the association's publications and in interviews. The one voice message was a call for action to save free enterprise in America from a "knock-out blow." The speech I used to deliver that message was called "Save The Frog"...

"Save the Frog"—A Message on Restoring Free Enterprise

"We hold these truths to be self-evident, that all Men are created equal. That they are endowed by their Creator, with certain unalienable rights. That among these are Life, Liberty, and the Pursuit of Happiness."

Life, liberty, and the pursuit of happiness, the words of our founding fathers, to describe those values most critical to the long-term success of this nation.

Life is short, and in addition to taking from life, we must give back to life. Liberty and freedom, two of the greatest attributes of this great nation, Liberty! Freedom! But greater than freedom itself as a country is America's ability to change. America's early history had a blackened eye because of slavery, but America had the ability to change and rise above slavery.

The pursuit of happiness. Didn't say a guarantee, didn't say it was in the contract, that you're gonna be happy. It simply said the opportunity to pursue happiness based upon each individual's desire to apply heart, mind, and back. The heart

*to have the passion to pursue happiness. The mind to decide
that you want to do it. And the back to work as hard as you
need to as long as you need to in order to achieve it. That was
the premise of our founding fathers. But somewhere along the
way, things kind of got off track. Things got a little bit off track
in terms of those values and those promises. And one of the big
differences today versus the early history of this country is that
our elected leaders back then, were part-time legislators and
full-time employers, citizens.* They had real jobs! *And when
they got through doing the legislative business, which was con-
fined to only a few months out of the year, they'd go back
home to their real jobs and relate to real people, talk about
real problems, look at real issues, talk about real opportunities,
and talk about real pursuit of happiness.*

*It was in the early thirties that America's greatness was
shocked with one of the lowest points in it's economic history.
All great countries go through some rise and some fall and
some decline. And it was in the 30s that this country experienced the Depression. And in an attempt to help those that
needed help the most, our government, being a passionate and
caring government, wanted to help those to get themselves out
of their economic situation. So it was in the early 30s that*
assistance programs *began in this country, starting with Social
Security assistance. And when it was originally put forth by the
legislators, it was intended to be an assistance mechanism for
those that retired after years of pursuing their happiness. And
back in 1930, even before they introduced Social Security
assistance, a well-intended program, the total cost of all government (federal, state, and local) was 10 percent of the Gross
Domestic Product, 10 percent. And of that 10 percent, three of
those percentage points were at the federal level; this was in
1930. So back in the thirties when America was showing its
compassion to help people, to give people a chance to pursue
happiness, we all contributed a little "bite out of our apple."
We all shared with those who didn't have as much as we have,
as a country. And these assistance programs continued to*

grow and grow. And back in 1935 when they first passed the Social Security Act, a well-intended program, we were paying 3 percent of payroll for all of our employees and then the employee was contributing 3 percent. Today, that number is more than double that. Why? Because in the last 60 years Social Security has gone from being something that is an assistance *program to a* dependency *program to an* entitlement *program. Entitlement programs weren't defined or even discovered or established in the thirties. They started as assistance, but they evolved to entitlement programs. And instead of our government today being 10 percent of our total Gross Domestic Product, today it's nearly 50 percent of our Gross Domestic Product, with 30 percentage points of that 50 percent going just to the federal level. That's 60 percent of all of the tax level revenue we pay being spent at the federal level today. It was only 30 percent back in 1930; today it's 60 percent.*

When Medicare started back in 1965 it was a well-intended assistance program. And our elected representatives told us it would cost six billion dollars to roll out and that in 25 years the cost would double, no more, it would be 12 billion dollars. But 25 years after 1965, the price tag was not 12 billion dollars, it was 107 billion dollars. A 900 percent miss! Oops, we were off by a few decimal points! Back in the early thirties there were no budget deficits. Isn't that a novel idea? There were no budget deficits. The deficits didn't start to grow until we started to allow assistance programs to evolve into entitlement programs. And instead of throwing out the programs that didn't work or modifying programs that needed to be modified, they just continue to grow and eat up more and more of our national revenue. And so today we talk, our legislators talk freely and often about the budget deficit. And the biggest debate going on in the United States Senate right now today, as I speak and as you listen, is on passing a bill that would force a balanced budget of the United States. This year the budget deficit, the amount we over spend, fell below 300 billion dollars. And if good things continue to happen in the economy it could get as low as 220 billion dollars. But if we do not change the growth in uncapped entitlement programs, if we as a country do not change our spending habits as a nation, it is estimated by the Year 2012, fact, entitlements, and interest on the debt, will consume all of our federal tax revenue. So that means we will not have any revenue remaining for defense. The Cold War is over, but you still have some maniacs out there in the world. We would have no money left for education, and many other of the discretionary programs if we do not change the course that we're on. And then in 1994, the Mother of all entitlement programs, Health Care Reform. A very noble and worthwhile objective, but a flawed, impractical approach. Because if that approach proposed by the administration had passed with mandates, mandates, mandates, it would have accelerated the bankruptcy date of the United States of America.

Well some people say, "How did we get into this mess?" And it is a mess. We allowed it to happen, because we elect them, and if we send them to Washington and we don't talk to them, guess what? They will do what is politically right rather than what is economically right. They will do what's good for the party, instead of what's good for the people. It's kind of like the old wives' tale, about the frog. If you take a frog and throw him in a pot of hot, boiling water the frog will jump out. But if you take the frog and put him in a pot of cold water (1935), gradually turn up the heat, little, by little, over a long period of time (60 years), little by little, the frog's body will adjust to that incremental increase of heat, and eventually boil to death. *The frog is free enterprise, that boiling heat that we feel as entrepreneurs and business people is the boiling bureaucracy of legislation, taxation, and regulation. As my friend Ted Fowler calls them, the "ations,"* we've been attacked by the "ations" and don't even realize that the heat's getting hotter.

In 1988, they said "Let's turn the heat up on the Restaurant

Association, let's see if we can't lower business meal deduct-
ibility from 100 percent to 80 percent and see if they notice."
And even as an industry, we protested this move because it's
simply an unfair tax on our industry, it's just unfair. But our
elected representatives, in their infinite wisdom said, "Well,
because of the fiscal crisis that we are faced with, we've got to
do this, but we won't bother you again." This was in 1988,
you've given at the office, so we won't be back to bother you on
this issue again.

In 1994, oops, up jumped the devil! Well, since you guys
adjusted so easily to a change from 100 percent to 80 percent,
well hell, let's take it to 50 percent. Because we need the
money. Why? Because this deficit is out of control. The only
thing we know to do is to throw more money at it. Our money!
So they moved it to 50 percent. So they turned the heat up just
a little bit more on the frog. Made it a little bit harder to start a
business. Made it a little bit tougher to stay in business in this
industry. And now there's a proposal by the Administration to
raise the minimum wage. I have nothing against people pursuing happiness, based upon their heart, their mind, and their
back. None of us do. But I have a problem with an unfunded
mandate on business. Which is what it is.

And secondly, just to show you the clarity of the logic that
we live with in our government, they're working on the wrong
problem. There are four million minimum wage workers in
America. Less than one million of them live in poverty house-
holds, which means the total income of the household is less
than $13,000 a year. There are 7.8 million people collecting
unemployment. There are nine million people on welfare. You
are an intelligent business person. Which problem should we
be working on? Jobs! And to make matters worse, under the
current welfare system, if a welfare person goes out and gets
one of these hamburger slinging jobs, as Secretary Reich calls
it, then they cut off their Medicaid assistance. That doesn't
make any sense. Something is wrong with the system. And so
we have allowed the water on the frog to get too hot.

But in 1994, America demonstrated one of its other greatest strengths. And that was it's ability once again to change. The unthinkable happened that the political pundits could not predict. That was November 8th. They changed the leadership in Congress, in both houses. Overnight. Shocked the political world and shocked this country. The American people demonstrated once again, the power of the ballot box still rules. And the new Congress and the new leadership has come in and they have said, "We are going to tell the American people the truth about the tragedy, the nature and the size of this problem. And it's going to be painful. But they can't do it without help from us, and encouragement from us to do what is right for this country long-term."

Not all of the people in Washington are bad guys, there are a lot of good guys, there are a lot of good ladies there. But they need the support and encouragement from the citizenry in order to be able to make the kinds of change that needs to be made.

So I encourage you, continue to believe that we can make a difference *because we did and we are.*

The second thing we can do about this. Make sure that as a business person, as an entrepreneur, that you do the basics. *Be a registered voter. Vote when it's time to vote. Encourage your employees to vote. Because one of the amazing things that happened in November 1994 was that even though the American people didn't read or understand all of the fine print, they developed a sense that something was going in the wrong direction and they responded. Our privilege and our freedom and our right to vote is one of the greatest privileges that we have in this country and when we do not vote, we risk losing that privilege. Let's do the basics. Contact your elected representatives periodically; they need to hear from you. And yes, it does make a difference.*

And number three, we have experienced 60 years of this boiling bureaucracy taking a bite out of our ability to pursue happiness. We've got to bite back. B*etter* I*mpact* T*he* E*lected.*

*By picking up a phone you can call your representatives and
say I agree with a balanced budget amendment. Why?
Because we have not as a country demonstrated that we have
the fiscal responsibility to do it without a hammer over our
head. We haven't done it. The biggest argument that many of
the opponents of a balanced budget amendment fear is that it
might tie the hands of government. Well, "no pepperoni" José.
Maybe their hands need to be tied so they can stop taking the
money out of my pocket and your pocket.*

*So yes, America is in a fiscal mess. But it is still the best
country in the world. And it is still one of the few countries in
the world that can go through the kind of change that we are
going through, and the kind of change that we've gone
through in the past and lived through it. Joseph Shumpeter, a
famous economist, wrote a book in 1942 called* Capitalism,
Socialism and Democracy. *And in his book, he stated that the
greatest threat to capitalism will not come from its failures, but
from it's success. And capitalism has been so successful we've
created a mess. And we've got to change it. It's still the greatest
country in the world that we can change; this is still the best
country in the world where you can be an entrepreneur.
Where you can be whatever you want to be, you can start
wherever you want to start, work as hard as you want to work.
Who would have thunk it, a young man from Atlanta,
Georgia, who had never heard of a pizza could end up running a pizza company one day. Who'd have thunk it! Only in
America because of our ability to pursue happiness.*

*You are the American entrepreneur. We represent that
entrepreneurial spirit. That is what this is about when we insist
on balancing the budget. That's what this is about when we
insist on turning down the heat on the frog. Restoring free
enterprise in America. Restoring the ability of people to dream
and be able to go and pursue those dreams. Because Rudyard
Kipling had it right when he said, "If you can fill life's unforgiving minute with 60 seconds of distance run." We're in a
race folks; we only have a minute to do it. And as Dr.*

*Benjamin E. Mays, who was the President of Morehouse
College when I attended there in the late 1960s, said, "It is not
a tragedy to not reach your goals, but it is a tragedy to have
no goals to reach. It's not a calamity to die with unfulfilled
dreams, but it is a calamity to have no dreams to fulfill." Let's
restore America's ability to dream, with Life, Liberty, and the
Pursuit of Happiness.*

The second initiative was called "B.I.T.E. Back," which was
designed to put some "teeth" into our influence with lawmakers, as
well as to demonstrate our collective clout as an industry. Too often
in the past we were put in a position of reacting to something after it
was already passed, due to the lack of a fast, industry-wide feedback
mechanism to lawmakers. As a result, one day while on an airplane
at 35,000 feet, I got the idea of a weekly phone call to thousands of
restaurateurs. I envisioned this call as little more than a brief update
on restaurant-related issues that were moving through Congress.
Immediately I became excited about the idea of thousands of our
members contacting their representatives and voicing their positions
on specific issues in a timely manner. Since the objective was to be
able to "**B**etter **I**mpact **T**he **E**lected" congressional leaders, I decided
to call the initiative "B.I.T.E. Back" to signify more "teeth" in our
efforts to influence Congress on behalf of free enterprise.

Each week I would record by phone from anywhere in the world
a "B.I.T.E. Back" message for the week. Members of the industry
would call our 1-800-NEWS NRA line and hear my message for the
week and my request for their help. Nearly 7,000 restaurateurs signed
up to participate, which generated about 1,000 calls per week to
Congress at critical times on critical issues. As one congressman told
me, "It only takes 15 calls on an issue to get their attention." Exhibit
4-3 is a sample "B.I.T.E. Back" message that received over 1,000 calls
for the week during the health care debate.

The "one voice" and "B.I.T.E. Back" initiatives worked to mobilize
and inspire many people to "do something." Coupled with the strong
history of the National Restaurant Association and a very competent

Exhibit 4-3 *Transcript of Herman Cain's B.I.T.E. Back Message for the Week of August 29–September 2, 1994*

Welcome to B.I.T.E. Back! This is Herman Cain, your President of the National Restaurant Association for the week of August 29, 1994.

I think Congress is beginning to get a message from the American people. Last week, I told you how the U.S. Senate was debating a 1,400-page health care bill that almost nobody had read. Senators started debating August 9th, and they kept going and going and they didn't get anywhere because they are working on a bill they can't fix. They could amend that bill until the cows come home and never begin to make it work. The American people understand that and I think it's beginning to dawn on Congress also, because on Thursday, the Senate called it quits and went home.

They say they will get back to work on health care in early September. Now they are at home doing what they should be doing . . . listening to the people. Now is the most important time for us to make sure they hear us loud and clear. Even though the media has concluded that there will be no health care bill this year, it is not for certain until Congress adjourns in October.

If you have not called your members of Congress within the last two weeks, call them today and inform them we want health care reform, but that we would rather have no health care bill than a bad bill. The wrong legislation on health care reform would be extremely dangerous to the future of this country.

If you are wondering whether your calls make a difference, yes they do! In fact, a staff member of one U.S. Senator actually called Elaine Graham of our Association staff and complained about all the calls as well as the effect of our campaign. She just said, "well, is he listening?" Obviously, he is. We are B.I.T.E.ing Back and thanks to all of you, it's working.

Thank you for calling and have an exceptionally wonderful week!

NRA staff, the enthusiastic support of fellow NRA board members, and many state restaurant associations, the "other NRA," as some in Washington, D.C., called us, became a strong, lead voice in the health care debate of 1994.

The NRA also took the leadership role in establishing a coalition of associations that shared our position. This allowed us to collectively voice our opposition to the Clinton plan to all members of Congress from many business sectors. The health care debate raging in Congress was intense, and we wanted to make sure many of the members were aware of the public and business sentiment about the *facts.* Specifically, *we felt the plan was a job killer, a bureaucracy builder and a non-solution to the wrong problem.* The president had even acknowledged in his State of the Union address that approximately nine out of ten people were already covered with health insurance. So, why not look for effective ways of providing access for the remaining ten percent while allowing market forces to bring the cost of health care down? As I told NBC news anchor Tom Brokaw during a network TV health care special, *"If I have a leak in the roof and I know that the roof is leaking, I don't blow up the building to fix the leak in the roof."*

One of our guest speakers at the NRA's annual public affairs conference held in Washington, D.C., in September 1994 was Senator Bob Packwood of Oregon. He was in the midst of his presentation to the more than 600 attendees from all over the country, when he was interrupted by one of his staff members who handed him a note. The senator paused, looked at the note, and then said to the audience, "Senator George Mitchell and the Democrats have thrown in the towel on the Clinton health care proposal."

The audience erupted into applause and leapt to a standing ovation. It was fortuitous timing because Bob Packwood had been one of the leading Republican senators opposing the President's proposal on "The Hill." I walked onto the stage and shook the senator's hand, saying, "Congratulations" (see the insert). He responded with, "We could not have done it without you and your people." At that moment I felt a tremendous sense of pride...we made a difference.

Who Is This Guy?!

The year I was President of the National Restaurant Association was by all measures a momentous year for our association in helping to shape public policy. Although many people in the restaurant industry knew of me because of my affiliation with Godfather's Pizza, Inc., most policymakers in Washington, D.C. were asking, "Who is this guy...where did he come from?"

When we completed our LBO in 1988 we realized then that the impact of outside legislative and regulatory forces on our ability to survive financially was intensifying. The restaurant industry had become a popular target of congressional initiatives to raise more revenue to feed that out-of-control federal spending appetite. Although GPI's financial projections of performance gave us room for an occasional "sneeze" without going into financial default with the bank, our business could not withstand the financial shock induced by external governmental mandates. In fact, we were less concerned about competitive forces than we were about potential legislative and regulatory forces.

When I joined the NRA board in 1988, I quickly gained a high level of respect for what it was about. I actively participated in whatever committees to which I was assigned with no aspirations about one day being president of the association...I genuinely wanted to make a contribution to the efforts of the industry and the NRA.

As time passed, my "three plus three" style attracted the respect of fellow board members and soon I was asked to be chairman of the Governmental Relations Committee. It is also one of the most challenging committees to lead because it is a committee of the full board which determines our legislative positions, priorities, and direction.

When I was asked to accept the nomination for treasurer of the NRA, to subsequently become vice president and president respectively, it was a major decision because of the time commitment required, especially during my year as president. Many NRA board members had encouraged me to accept the nomination because they felt that I could make a difference to the industry, especially given the growing intensification of the "ations" on businesses such as

Godfather's. Even though GPI is perceived as a big corporation by some, we are actually a system of smaller independent businesses where many of our franchisees have less than five units. These types of businesses are usually the hardest hit by intrusive legislation and unnecessary regulations.

Before I became CEO of GPI, I was not as aware of how free enterprise in the U.S. was being discouraged by our ever-growing federal bureaucracy and deficit spending. I was not as aware until I experienced how day-to-day business decisions are so dependent upon legislative, regulatory, and taxation concerns.

Please do not misunderstand where I am coming from. The U.S. is the greatest country in the world for achieving one's dreams, and we are also one of the most giving countries. When well-intended public assistance programs started in the 1930s, few people imagined they would grow into a sea of dysfunctional entitlement programs of the 1990s.

When I accepted the nomination to become President of the National Restaurant Association in 1992, I never imagined that I would be leading the restaurant industry during the debate on the "mother of all entitlement programs" in 1994…Clinton's health care proposal.

Leadership Observations

Chapter 1 discusses the three *critical* characteristics a leader must possess and the three *critical* things a leader must do…"three plus three" leadership. During the town hall meeting described in this chapter, President Clinton displayed "two plus one" of the "three plus three" principles.

As someone who sought and won the "highest office in the land," Mr. Clinton is obviously self-motivated *(D-factor)* and a risk taker *(E-factor)*. The well-intended objective of providing health insurance for the ten percent of our citizens without coverage is evidence of attempting to be an entrepreneurial problem solver, but his proposed solution fell way short of being the right alternative. I do not believe he showed great focus *(F-factor),* because his proposal was to "blow up the building to fix the leak in the roof," and then attempt to convince the public that this was the right strategy.

Two of the critical things a leader must do, President Clinton did not do. First, leaders "look, listen, learn, and then lead," and to *lead* is defining the right problem, asking the right questions, selecting the right alternative, and achieving the desired results. Although the president reportedly launched his series of town hall meetings to "listen" to the American people, it was clear that the real objective was to "convince." Hundreds of people that wrote to me or called after the broadcast made the same observation.

Just consider, for example, the fact that he tried to convince me that his incorrect math was correct. The other problem in trying to "convince" rather than listen was the implication that he knew more about my business dynamics than I did, when he said "just raise your prices" to pay for the cost of his health care proposal. Listening is an integral part of a leader's ability to select the right alternative *if* he is working on the right problem.

The other critical thing that the president did not do during this town hall meeting was *remove barriers* to motivation. He had hoped that the town hall meeting would motivate more people to get behind his proposal, but it did just the opposite. The complexity of his proposal was a barrier, the cost of his proposal was a barrier, the envisioned bureaucracy of his plan was a barrier, and the impact on jobs which was illuminated by my question to him was a barrier. None of these barriers were removed, but instead, other barriers were created.

When the President could not refute my comment that "his calculations were incorrect," it suggested that maybe the administration had not done its "homework"...that's a barrier. When it was later revealed that there was no representation by a businessperson on the task force that developed the proposal...that's a barrier. When it became obvious that the president's proposal was not working on the right problem...that's a real big barrier. The leader is responsible for challenging his people to give him correct information, and for the makeup of the task force or committee developing the proposal. And if the leader does not make certain that he or she and his or her people are working on the *right problem*, there is no way one can select the right alternative and achieve the desired results.

The president did not *remove barriers* and he did not *lead* as defined in the context of this book. He did, however, *inspire* those people who were already predisposed in favor of his plan. Many of those that were undecided or already opposed to his plan "spoke out" and "spoke up"—all the way to the U.S. Congress.

The Leak in the Roof

People want their leaders to be human...up to a point. When the president said to me, "Let me ask you a favor, would you send to me, personally, your calculations?" I sincerely believed the president was interested in following up on our discussion, so I sent him my calculations. My disappointment afterwards was not the fact that he did not personally respond to me, but that his lieutenant's follow-up letter dodged the key issue—the president's arithmetic was wrong, leading to faulty assumptions and worse yet, faulty conclusions. I had hoped the president and his staff would have taken a serious second look at their conclusions about the cost and impact of the health care plan, because after all, his plan was being presented to the American people as a "cure all" for health care with no side effects. But on the other hand, maybe they did revisit their arithmetic and did not like what they found. I guess we will never know. People still ask me, "Did the president ever get back to you?" The answer is no, but I received a letter from one of his people which never addressed the president's calculations, my calculations, or my question.

I do not like to criticize without offering an alternative suggestion. So, if I had had an opportunity to provide some input on attacking the health care issue before "the train left the station," I would have suggested a national campaign which would (1) encourage preventive care, (2) demonstrate that we *all* pay, and (3) demonstrate what we *all* can do to reduce the system costs. The biggest problem with our health system is not the quality of our medical care, but the public attitude that health care is "health care." It is not "health care," it is "sick care" because many people *don't care* until they get sick. This mindset is the result of years of public and private conditioning that if you have health care insurance then you are not paying for your "sick care" when you get sick. In fact, we are all paying for it and the cost of medical care abuses. We must first change the national mindset before we change behavior.

The national campaign, in conjunction with some changes in the tax treatment of insurance premiums, and in conjunction with the natural forces of free enterprise would make insurance more affordable and accessible for everyone. The 90 percent of the public who have insurance would be happier and the 10 percent of the public without insurance would have a better opportunity to obtain insurance. The "leak in the roof" would now be much smaller and fixable instead of continuing to grow faster than we could replace the "roof shingles."

National campaigns to change our national attitude about issues have worked well in the past. The best example I can recall is the "Keep America Beautiful" campaign headed by Lady Bird Johnson in the 1960s. To this day millions of Americans would not even think about throwing trash out of the window of a car.

If we had attacked the right problem concerning our health care system, then I and many others could have fought passionately *for* something instead of against something. I believe we could have fixed the "leak in the roof."

The Lightning Rod

People want to feel a strong sense of trust in their leader. When General Colin Powell was considering running for president but finally decided that he would not, millions of Americans, including myself, were disappointed. Most people that wanted him to run were disappointed because he is perceived to be, and has proven himself to be, a leader that people feel they can trust.

Hundreds of people have told me, either in person or via letter, that my town hall meeting "chat" with President Clinton *inspired* them to do something. Many people indicated that they ended up writing and expressing their viewpoints on this matter to their Congressperson, although at one time they had thought that writing would not matter. Others made that phone call to their elected officials, although once before they believed their input would not be heard. Some told me that because of what I had done, they maintained hope that something could be done to stop a government plan that millions of people did not believe in. Many people shared firsthand experiences they had had with similar plans in other countries. One particularly touching letter was from a lady who described the nationalized health care in her native country as so bad, that the government does not know how to undo the situation.

When I attended that town hall meeting telecast, it was not my intent, or hope, that I would inspire millions of other people to do something. Nor did I go to the telecast thinking that I would be a voice for small business or a "lightning rod" for the health care debate. I simply wanted to provide some constructive input about my business, my industry, and the right problem.

I do not believe that I was the first person who tried to point out to the president and members of his administration how his proposed plan would impact jobs and the economy. So, what was it about that "four minutes of notoriety" that inspired so many people and became the "turning point of the debate" as Speaker of the House Newt Gingrich called it? (See Appendix C for a list of references.)

My own assessment of what people saw in that town hall meeting was, firstly, a calm and confident businessman who sounded like he knew what he was talking about without sounding arrogant or disrespectful. I certainly was not the typical image of a ruthless, big business corporate executive who would challenge the president.

Secondly, I believe the simplicity of my question ("What do I tell all those people whose jobs I will have to eliminate?") was one to which many people could relate and understand, and thus, it reflected their own concerns. That question also put clearly on the table the issue of how much the Clinton plan would cost—a subject the president and his administration had consistently tried to downplay.

Thirdly, millions of people feared that the Clinton health care plan would become just another *well-intended*, but out-of-control, social program such as Social Security and Medicare. Like these, it would require more and more taxes and place an even greater burden on our overall economy. But worse, people had lost hope that they could have much impact on the outcome...up until then.

Leadership is not an endowed consequence of positionship, just as singing ability is not an endowed consequence of having a voice. The "stuff" that people see in a leader is not always quantifiable or immediately recognizable, but they know it when they see it and they know when it is missing.

The health care debate of 1994 was missing something up until "The Attack of the Hermanator."

SUCCESS IS A JOURNEY

"THE MAN IN THE ARENA"

The credit belongs to the man who is actually in the arena, whose face is marred by dust and sweat and blood, who knows the great enthusiasms, the great devotions, and spends himself in a worthy cause; who at best, if he wins, knows the thrills of high achievement, and, if he fails, at least fails daring greatly, so that his place shall never be with those cold and timid souls who know neither victory nor defeat.

John F. Kennedy on Theodore Roosevelt
New York City, December 5, 1961

When I lost that 7th grade election for president of the student body I did not feel very successful. Fortunately, I got over it and learned that success is not measured by a single event, nor is it something which can be achieved in the "twinkling of an eye." I also learned that success is determined more by what's inside of you than what's around you. I learned these lessons from the first "great leader" I knew—my dad, Luther Cain, Jr.

Half a House

My father's journey started when he left home around the age of 18 to find work in the city. He, his parents, and eleven brothers and sisters all lived in a small three-room house on a small farm in Arlington, Tennessee. He literally left home with just the clothes on his back determined (motivated) to build a better life than that of his father, the constant struggle as a small farmer just to survive.

He found work at a tire manufacturing plant in Mansfield, Ohio, where he and my mother met and were married. Eventually ending up in Atlanta, my father worked three jobs at one point *(E-factor)* in order to save enough money for a down payment on a house. He wanted to move his family out of that "half a house," which was three rooms of a six-room duplex where we lived most of my years before I entered the 8th grade. He worked as a chauffeur for the Coca-Cola Company, a barber, and a night custodian for a Pillsbury dough plant located in Atlanta. Little did I know that my journey would take me through The Pillsbury Company when I worked with my dad as his helper at the Pillsbury plant.

As my father's "blue-collar career" started to take off, he was selected as the chauffeur and valet for the CEO of the Coca-Cola

Company. This job required long hours and most days away from home, causing him to only work that one job. When he did have time off it was usually on Sunday, when he could go to church with the family.

In church, when he became a deacon it was not long before he was asked to become chairman of the Deacon Board. When he joined the choir, it was not long before he ended up president of the choir, or as lead singer in the choir, displaying his natural gift of "stage presence." He was not only the head of our family, but he was also the leader of our extended family and among his friends. Many people came to him when they were down on their luck or in trouble, and many would seek his great common sense advice. You could say that he was "The Godfather."

Dad's dream (focus) was to be able to buy a "whole house." The summer before I started 8th grade, my dad came home one day and told my mother, my brother, and me to get in the car, that we were going for a ride. He drove to a suburb west of Atlanta and pulled up in front of a small six-room all-brick house and said, "This is our new house." We were surprised! We now had a whole house. Dad was always working towards something even after he bought the new house. He worked to help my brother and me with college expenses, and then he worked to "put a little something away" for retirement.

Luther Cain, Jr. never allowed a lack of formal education to be a *barrier* to his success. He never used his starting point in life or the racial conditions of his time as excuses for failing to pursue his dreams. My father had a naturally competitive spirit which motivated him when he felt like he was "the only man in the arena," but he always maintained compassion for other people. Dad's journey taught me the value of having dreams, the motivation to pursue those dreams, and the determination to achieve them.

A Seed of Corn

I learned a lot about life and leadership from my father without consciously realizing at the time that those lessons would shape what's inside of me. Many of the qualities I inherited from my dad started to show up when I was in high school.

I joined the high school band in the 8th grade even though I had never played an instrument in my life. When I met with the band director, Mr. Terry, he asked what instrument I wanted to learn to play. I then asked him what he needed most, and he said that he was short of trombone players, so I learned to play the trombone. By 9th grade I had advanced from 3rd part last chair (the worst player) to 2nd part first chair (better than five other trombone players). When I started 10th grade I was trombone section leader...first part, first chair. When I started my junior year I was also selected student director, the first time a junior had been chosen for that coveted responsibility.

Our high school band was very competitive and Mr. Terry taught us the "thrill of victory" through hard work, discipline, practice, and the pride within us. He constantly told us we could outplay any band in the state of Georgia if we wanted to, and he made sure we wanted to, as we consistently scored superior or outstanding at high school band contests.

The experience in the band taught me to appreciate what's required for the collective success of a group, which helped the pride, motivation, and confidence already inside of me to grow. Just as a seed of corn needs fertile soil, water, and sunshine to grow to its plentiful harvest, *success starts inside and must be cultivated with encouragement and accomplishment to prevent the growth of "weeds" of doubt.*

My high school math teacher, Mr. Johnson, also cultivated my confidence, but more importantly, he inspired me to begin to dream big dreams. He did this in the classroom by helping me to become a good student of mathematics, and with his words of encouragement.

One Saturday during my 10th grade year, Mr. Johnson asked me to help him wax and shine his car for a few dollars. The whole time we were there in Lincoln Park not far from where I lived, I kept wondering how many dollars was a "few dollars" but I was not about to ask. As we talked while we worked during those several hours, Mr. Johnson made a riveting comment that still rings in my memory today: "Herman Cain, you can be whatever you want to be if you *work a little harder* and *work a little longer."*

Up until that point in my life I had only thought about being a teacher or a preacher because those were the two white-collar professions I had been exposed to directly. My mother and father had always encouraged me to be "something," but they never told me what to be. When Mr. Johnson started telling me I could be "whatever I wanted to be" my thinking was elevated. Things that I had only seen on television as something that other people achieved started me to ponder just what I did want to be other than a teacher or a preacher. Mr. Johnson inspired me to begin to dream big dreams of not just a "few dollars" but one day, some "big dollars."

I graduated from high school as salutatorian (second highest grade point average) of my class. This achievement was the result of the nurturing love of my mother, the competitive spirit inherited from my father, the experience of winning from Mr. Terry, the possibility of achieving big dreams from Mr. Johnson, and the encouragement and genuine concern of all the teachers and staff at Samuel Howard Archer High School. Wanting to achieve academic excellence was not my motivation nor a concept to which I could relate.

But I could relate to one day making $20,000 a year in a "good job." That was my "big dollar dream," because that was twice as much money as I could imagine and twice as much as I needed to qualify for a credit card. To reach that dream I knew I had to go to college, which I had learned would cost a lot of money. My father told me that he would help me as much as he could, but we knew it would not be easy.

At that point, I focused on selecting a college in Atlanta so I could commute from home. Mr. Johnson suggested Morehouse College because it was one of the best colleges in the country that just happened to be in Atlanta. I was accepted to Morehouse and offered a first-year tuition scholarship...I took it.

The House

When I entered Morehouse College in 1963 I was not familiar with its tradition, its legacy of well-known and accomplished alumni, nor with the man who built Morehouse into a great institution, Dr. Benjamin E. Mays.

Dr. Benjamin E. Mays "filled life's unforgiving minute with sixty seconds of distance run" while President of Morehouse College. For 27 years he *inspired* young black men to reach beyond their grasp and to pursue great goals despite their starting point or their current circumstances. He built a college so well respected for its academics and the accomplishments of its graduates that Morehouse was described as the Harvard of the South. But, Dr. Mays pointed out in a speech I heard him give that the description was wrong...Harvard is the Morehouse of the North.

Dr. Mays was a leader of exceptional *focus*. He insisted that faculty members pursue their Ph.D. degrees in their respective disciplines, and he would never compromise academics at Morehouse for any extracurricular pursuits. During my four years as a student at Morehouse our football team won very few games but it did not seem to dampen the attitude of the student body. I played in the marching band and had to watch this for four years! Dr. Mays attended most of the games with his wife, Sadie, and always seemed proud of the team's efforts despite the losses. But during his weekly address to the students he would go right back to pounding away on his favorite themes...academic excellence and achievement.

Dr. Mays instilled in us a great sense of pride that many have called the "Morehouse mystique." He challenged us intellectually and spiritually and always with a passion you could hear in his voice and see in his eyes. His persona on campus was like a respected father figure who only needed to give a stern glance to discourage unruly behavior. He spoke often of the impressive achievement of Morehouse's graduates seasoned with historical reminders of where they started and the struggles we too would one day face as we tried to make our mark. One of Morehouse's most distinguished graduates, Dr. Martin Luther King, Jr. described Dr. Mays as his "spiritual mentor" and his "intellectual father." This is true of all those who experienced his leadership as a student at Morehouse College.

Even though I graduated from high school as salutatorian of my class, I struggled as a student at Morehouse. Most of my classmates were much better prepared academically as reflected in their SAT scores, and the curriculum and classes were very demanding. I started to realize why Morehouse had the reputation it had, and that if I were going to graduate, I needed to…"work a little harder and work a little longer."

I decided to major in mathematics because that was my strongest subject, and that's what Mr. Johnson had recommended. He had told me that since I was not sure exactly what profession I wanted to pursue, mathematics would give me the discipline, reasoning, and quantitative skills to pursue whatever I decided. Realizing that those four years at "The House" were going to be tough academically, I was determined that I would maintain at least a "B" average in my major, so I would have something positive to accentuate when I graduated and started looking for a job.

I also sang in the Morehouse College Glee Club because of my interest in singing and the fact that the glee club went on a two-week spring tour every year to cities across the country. The only place I had been outside of Atlanta was Arlington, Tennessee, to visit my father's family on that small dusty farm where he grew up. So, a two-week tour with the glee club sounded exciting. Only 40 members of the 100-voice glee club would go on the annual tour, for which we had to audition each year. I made it all four years at Morehouse, and was also chosen as a member of the college quartet my senior year. The glee club was another experience of unsurpassed excellence under the direction of Dr. Wendel P. Whalum. Its performances were captivating, a tradition which it still maintains today. The glee club honored me during my senior year by selecting me as its president.

In 1967 I graduated from Morehouse, also the year Dr. Mays retired as its president. He gave the commencement address and received an honorary doctorate degree from the school he had given his life to build.

My father encouraged me to "be something," and Mr. Johnson

encouraged me to dream big dreams. Dr. Mays and my Morehouse experience compelled me to achieve *great* dreams...all from a seed inside of me.

Whole New World

When I graduated from Morehouse in 1967 I had received no less than 25 "good" job offers from all over the country. It was not because I was a stellar student with a high grade point average, but because I had a "B" average in my major (mathematics) and I learned to interview well and how to project that "Luther Cain, Jr." personality. The other reason I received so many job offers was the fact that there was more pressure in the late 60s to hire more blacks, women, and minorities as a result of the Civil Rights Act of 1964.

I accepted my first "good job" with the Naval Weapons Laboratory of the Department of the Navy (DON) (the name has changed since then) in Dahlgren, Virginia. The job offer was not the one offering the most money, but it had a program for obtaining a master's degree if your job performance was high and you were able to qualify for the program. I was hired as a mathematician (general schedule) GS-7 making $7,729.00 a year, and I had no idea what an applications mathematician did in a typical day. I was really nervous that the first day on the job they would ask me to prove one of those mathematical theories I had missed on an exam during college...they did not...whew!

This was a whole new world. It was the first time I had ever lived away from home, my first time living in another town, my first time working in an office with my own assigned desk, and my first workplace experience where 95 percent of the people were white. My high school was all black, and Morehouse was an all-black school except for a few exchange students.

I was assigned to a department called exterior ballistics. This group was responsible for analyzing data and determining aerodynamic coefficients for all Navy projectiles...missiles, bombs, and bullets...using the equations of motion. My job was to apply a computer simulation model to real-time data measurements on a new or modified projectile, deriving the "numbers" that could be programmed into an on-board fire control computer. This allowed the battleship or fighter aircraft to improve its target "hit" ratio. That's what I did in a typical day.

The Haircut

I grew up in the segregated South and witnessed the evolution to desegregation. I experienced segregated buses, segregated water fountains, movie theaters, and public facilities of all types, but was also able to experience them when they were no longer legally segregated. So when I got to Dahlgren, Virginia, and experienced overt discrimination "revisited" I was shocked. Naive is probably a better description.

Dahlgren was so small we had to go 26 miles to Fredericksburg, Virginia, to buy groceries, go to a movie, and even get a haircut. On my first weekend in town I drove to Fredericksburg to get some groceries and a haircut. I stopped at the first barber shop I saw where I could see black barbers working inside. I figured they would have more experience at cutting my hair the way I wanted it cut. I went inside and took a seat in the waiting area, as I would have at a barber shop in Atlanta, until the next available barber could cut my hair. As I sat there for about 30 minutes, I noticed that they kept taking the white customers before me, even if they came in after me.

I finally went up and asked one of the barbers why they had not called me up to get my hair cut yet, and he said they were not allowed to cut black folks' hair in this shop. I asked what would happen if he did, and he said he would lose his job at that shop. He then gave me directions to the barber shop in the black section of Fredericksburg where I could get my hair cut. Not wanting to jeopardize this man's livelihood I left the shop, bought my groceries at a grocery store about two blocks away, then drove back to Dahlgren. I had not felt that humiliated since the day in 1958 when my friends and I were riding the city bus home from high school and the driver told us to move to the back of the bus so the white passengers could sit down. If we did not, he was going to call the police.

After that barber shop incident I bought some hair clippers to cut my own hair, and I have been cutting it myself ever since.

A Dream Come True

Discrimination on the job was much more covert and sometimes subtle. There was a guy that started in our work unit the same time I did. He was white with a master's degree, and I was black without a master's degree. At the end of our first year we both had achieved "outstanding" quarterly ratings for our respective assignments, and we were doing the same level of work. With such high ratings we were both promoted to GS-9 after 12 months on the job. We both continued to perform "outstandingly" the next 12 months, and he was promoted to GS-11 in exactly 12 months but my promotion was effective in 13 months. When I asked my boss why, he said it was because he had a master's degree. This one-month lag continued the following year so I decided to "remove" a barrier my boss had in evaluating my performance—I decided to get a master's degree.

It took me three years of applying for the graduate fellowship program and still being rated outstanding on the job before I was finally approved. I decided to go to Purdue University for a master's in computer science. My boss told me I probably would not be able to get in...but I did. He also told me I would not be able to maintain the necessary 3.0 GPA for master's work...but I did. In fact, I finished the master's program in two semesters and one summer at Purdue in Lafayette, Indiana, with a 3.4 GPA.

Shortly after I returned back to my work unit, my boss decided to leave DON. His boss was the head of the department consisting of several hundred people, and had to select someone to be the new GS-13 supervisory work unit manager. The two internal candidates were the "other guy" that started in the work unit when I did, and me. We both had the same years of experience including graduate school time, we both had performed consistently outstanding in our respective jobs and *now* we both had master's degrees. Throughout all those years, my "people skills" had been recognized, even by my retiring boss, as being better than the other guy's. I was promoted to that GS-13 supervisory position which paid $20,001 per year in 1972...a dream come true!

When my boss had tried to discourage me, I became more determined that I would succeed at getting my master's degree. It certainly was not an easy year at Purdue because just as it was when I entered Morehouse, the other students were much better prepared going into the program. I simply "worked a little harder" and much longer study hours.

The overt discrimination at the barber shop and the covert discrimination on the job were just a continuation of history that I thought was over after the changes I had lived through growing up in Atlanta. Martin Luther King, Jr.'s message of non-violent protesting still rang loud and clear in my mind. When they would not cut my hair I protested by learning to cut it myself. When my advancement was delayed because I didn't have a master's degree, I earned one and did it convincingly. Although it took patience, I decided to become unquestionably better than the "other guy."

The color of my skin has never been a *barrier* to performance or success inside of me, but it has sometimes been a barrier to others around me. Performance which exceeds expectations is the best response to biases or ill-informed attitudes.

No Vacancy

My five and a half years at the DON was certainly a "success" by most standards. I had moved up rapidly, reached my goal of $20,000 a year, had earned my master's degree, was working in air conditioning (which is what my mother considered a "good job"), had gotten married, had a daughter and was buying a house for the first time, had earned four weeks of vacation a year, and I was managing a group of professionals...life was good, and I was only 27 years old.

It became apparent after working as a GS-13 work unit leader for a while that moving up to a GS-14 was more a function of time than opportunity. That's when I started to explore making a career change. I really had no clue as to what I might be able to transfer my experience and skills toward, so I started reading business magazines looking for ideas. Since I had been working in a highly specialized and technical profession, "corporate America" seemed like a whole new world.

Eventually, I sent my resume to a number of corporations which seemed to be good companies. The only one that responded with a request to interview me was the Coca-Cola Company headquartered in Atlanta, my home town. That's when I met Bob Copper who told me that, quite frankly, they were interviewing me as a courtesy because my father worked as the chauffeur for the CEO, and that they really did not have a job vacancy available.

I thanked him for being honest and he took me to lunch anyway, where we got acquainted and talked about what I had done while at the DON. About two weeks later I received a call that his boss wanted to interview me. I asked, "for what," since they did not have a job, and he told me that he was trying to get approval for another position in his department because I had exceeded his expectations. When I asked what he had expected he said that he had not expected me to have a master's degree from Purdue University because he knew the program was tough, and that what I had achieved at the DON took "smarts" and tenacity. I was the kind of person he needed to help his department and the Coca-Cola Company.

I went back for the second interview and received an offer to become a group manager of management science reporting to Bob Copper. I accepted because it offered the excitement of the unknown and an opportunity not to be limited by time in grade. I also got the wild idea that maybe I could become a vice president for somebody, somewhere, doing something, someday.

Never Look Back

At each destination point on my journey, I was always faced with the decision to take the risk of a new opportunity or stay comfortably where I was at the time. Sometimes I went looking for the opportunity and sometimes it found me. It's like standing at a bus stop. If you get on the bus when a new opportunity comes along you don't know exactly where it will end up. If you stay where you are, you never know when the next bus will come along. In either case, you never look back.

Success is about having the motivation to want to succeed, the entrepreneurial tenacity to navigate through its treacherous detours, and the focus to keep your eye toward the next destination. Success is about removing barriers that you encounter and withstanding those that you may not even know are there, asking the right questions along the way, selecting the right alternatives, and then making it happen with exceptional value-added determination.

At the Department of the Navy I overcame the barrier of "color" in the minds of others. At the Coca-Cola Company I overcame the barrier of "low expectations" from others. At The Pillsbury Company I overcame the barrier of being the "young whipper-snapper." At Burger King I overcame the barrier of being the "old dude" from Pillsbury, and the barrier that others wanted me to fail. At Godfather's I overcame the barrier of disbelief that we could "yank victory from the jaws of defeat." In the health care debate of 1994, I simply asked the right question.

Success is a journey, not a destination. My journey has exceeded all my expectations. I never looked back, and I never rode in the back of the "bus" because I never wanted to miss my next destination. It's been quite a ride so far!

CHAPTER 6

LIVE YOUR DREAMS

Dream

Land of the Free

It's Your Life

If you can dream and not make dreams your master;
If you can think and not make thoughts your aim;
If you can meet with triumph and disaster
And treat those two impostors just the same;
If you can bear to hear the truth you've spoken
Twisted by knaves to make a trap for fools,
Or watch the things you gave your life to broken,
And stoop to build 'em up with worn-out tools;

If you can talk with crowds and keep your virtue,
or walk with kings—nor lose the common touch;
If neither foes nor loving friends can hurt you;
If all men count with you, but none too much;
If you can fill the unforgiving minute
with sixty seconds worth of distance run—
Yours is the Earth and everything that's in it,
And—which is more—you'll be a man, my son!

Rudyard Kipling

* paragraphs two and four

Leading your life to live your dreams is "three plus three" leadership of yourself. Your dreams define what you are about, and what you are motivated to do *(D-factor)*. Your individual risk index *(E-factor)* determines your level of focus in going after your dreams *(F-factor)*.

When your dreams are *your dreams* then you can deal with the *barriers* that will inevitably get in your way. Some barriers you may choose not to remove, and some barriers are not removable at all. In either case, you find a way to go over, under, or around the barrier. If you live your dreams then barriers are setbacks and not permanent detours. Barriers are timing delays but not cancellations of your journey.

When you *ask the right questions* of yourself you improve your chances of making the right decision (selecting the right alternative) to achieve your desired outcome. Your *inspiration* comes from your own self-motivation plus the encouragement of those around you. If you do not feel you are leading your life to live your dreams, your "three plus three" could be adding up incorrectly.

Dream

Anyone can dream but not everyone embraces their dreams. To embrace your dreams is to want them badly enough that you are willing to work hard enough and long enough to reach them. When you run into detours along the way or experience setbacks, the passion inside of you gives you the strength to pick yourself up again, shake the dust off your feet, and keep going.

Dreams do not always have to be big or grand or capable of

changing millions of people. Dreams come in all sizes, shapes, forms, and descriptions, and are divinely inspired as a signal that *your life is on the right track.* Your dreams do not have to be aimed at changing the world as long as they are aimed at "what you love, what you do, and what you hope for"—happiness.

Dreams that touch one child and make a difference in that child's life may one day touch millions or even change the world. And just as only God knows how many apples there are in an apple seed, only He knows how many people will be touched by your good deed.

One of my contemporary heroes is Dr. Robert Schuller, Pastor of the Crystal Cathedral Ministries of Garden Grove, California. He is a leader of hearts, minds, and souls. His dream to build the world's largest and most successful television ministry is unsurpassed. He started his church in a drive-in theater in Southern California. I first heard of Dr. Schuller in the 1970s while working at The Pillsbury Company, when my boss at the time gave me a copy of Dr. Schuller's book entitled *Move Ahead With Possibility Thinking.* His story and his words helped inspire me to dream beyond even those dreams I once thought were too big. How else would a young dreamer of humble beginnings, who happens to be black, dare to dream of becoming a "president of something, for somebody, somewhere?"

As Dr. Mays wrote, "It isn't a calamity to die with dreams unfulfilled, but it is a calamity not to dream."

Land of the Free

We are fortunate that we live in a country where dreams *can* come true. The "pursuit of happiness" is not only a right, it is an obligation. Our Creator did not put us here to be unhappy or not to dream. Our great country faces many complex and challenging problems in need of redefinition and refocusing. I believe that the solutions to even our most complex problems are within our grasp if we are working on the right problems, and there are enough people who believe we must solve those problems. Our country has demonstrated time and again that it can solve any problem to which it puts its collective

Godfather's Pizza, Inc. Registered Trademark in 1983

Godfather's Pizza, Inc. Registered Trademark as Implemented in 1988

Godfather's Pizza, Inc. Internal Logo During the Turnaround Years

The Hit Godfather's Will Take Under Clinton's Health Care Plan

Annualized from Jan. 1994 data	HOURS	WAGES
975 full-time employees	1,915,742	$18,671,075
1,570 part-time employees who work 10+ hours a week	1,537,983	$8,011,091
720 employees who work less than 10 hours a week	221,125	$1,115,347
153 employees on leave of absence/other	0	0
3,418 TOTAL EMPLOYEES	**3,674,850**	**$27,797,513**

Under Current Health Insurance Plan
594 employees are eligible
409 participate

Current cost of plan:	**$540,758**
Potential cost of Clinton plan: (cap of 7.9% of payroll)	**$2,196,604**
Additional Cost:	**$1,655,246**

Source: Godfather's Pizza, Inc.

The graphic that accompanied Herman Cain's
letter to President Clinton as it appeared
in the *Wall Street Journal*
(the letter can be found on pages 125–126).

Winston R. Wallin
Chairman and CEO, Medtronics, Inc.
(formerly President and COO, The Pillsbury Company)

Herman Cain and Senator Bob Packwood
at the National Restaurant Association during the announcement
of the end to the 1994 Health Care Debate.

Luther Cain, Jr.
Herman Cain's Father and "Hero"

Dr. Benjamin E. Mays
Late President Emeritus, Morehouse College, Atlanta, GA

desire, as long as we are working on the right problem and we have the right leadership to get us there.

The **federal budget deficit** which threatens our economy is a problem of shared sacrifices, not a problem of raising more taxes. The problem with our current **income tax law** is that it had no *focus* in 1913 when it first became law and now it has evolved into a seven million word "mess"...throw it out and start over! The problem with our **welfare system** is that it pays people not to work...let's pay them to work and eventually many of them will work themselves off of welfare. **Youth violence** and drug abuse is not a problem in the streets, it is a problem in the home...hold parents responsible. More focus on **education** is not the problem, the *focus* of education is the problem...teach everyone the basics first. **Racial prejudice** is not a problem of the "head" but a problem of the "heart"...open hearts will create open minds. We have not lost our **moral values** as a nation, we have simply forgotten the value of our morals.

It is not only up to the occasional "great leaders" that come along in our lifetime, like John F. Kennedy or Martin Luther King, Jr., it is up to all of us to help redefine and refocus our nation's problems so *we* can begin to solve them. In doing so, we will help "good leaders" achieve great things for us all.

It's Your Life

Life is about choices. People may not choose to be motivated, risk takers, or even focused (*D, E, F*). But people do choose to remove barriers to their happiness or just leave things as they are. People do choose to lead their lives for what they believe in or to lead their lives for something else. People do choose to live their life with vigor and enthusiasm or with "those cold and timid souls who know neither victory nor defeat" *(remove, lead, inspire)*.

Leading your life is about making choices and living with them. That's why the choices you make should point toward your dreams.

I am blessed that my wife and I chose to live our lives together because *together* we have achieved our dreams of a comfortable lifestyle, the joys and frustrations of parenting, more laughter than tears, and more blessings to give back to life. I am thankful that God gave us a journey filled with adventure, manageable *barriers,* and many rewarding destinations.

We were all put here on this earth by our Creator to "make a difference" in the *minute* He has given each of us on His timeline of eternity. I am thankful for the first 50 years of my *minute,* my father's *minute* of 56 years, my mother's *minute* of 70 years and counting, and my maternal grandmother's *minute* of 100 years and still going.

Your *minute* is "forced upon you, can't refuse it, didn't seek it, didn't choose it, but it's up to you to use it."

Lead your life to live your dreams…it's your *minute* and it's your life!

"GOD'S MINUTE"

I've only just a minute,
Only sixty seconds in it.
Forced upon me, can't refuse it,
Didn't seek it, didn't choose it,
But it's up to me to use it.
I must suffer if I lose it,
Give an account if I abuse it.
Just a tiny little minute,
But eternity is in it.

Anonymous

APPENDIXES

APPENDIX A

Leadership History

1988–Present   Chairman and CEO, Godfather's Pizza, Inc.

1995–Present   Board of Directors, Nabisco

1991–Present   Board of Directors, SuperValu, Inc.

1992–Present   Board of Directors, UtiliCorp United, Inc.

1992–Present   Board of Directors, Whirlpool Corporation

1992–Present   Board of Directors, Omaha Chamber of Commerce

1988–Present   Board of Directors, Edmonson Youth Outreach Program, Omaha, Nebraska

1995–1997   Chairman of the Board, Federal Reserve Bank of Kansas City, MO (10th District)

1994–1995   Chairman of the Board and President, National Restaurant Association

1986–1988   President, Godfather Pizza, Inc., as a subsidiary of The Pillsbury Company

1982–1986   Vice President and Regional General Manager, Philadelphia Region, Burger King Corporation

1980–1982   Vice President of Systems and Services, The
Pillsbury Company

1979–1980   Director of Management Information Systems,
Consumer Products Division, The Pillsbury
Company

1978–1979   Director of Corporate Business Analysis, The
Pillsbury Company

1977–1978   Manager of Corporate Business Analysis, The
Pillsbury Company

1973–1977   Manager of Management Science, The Coca-Cola
Company

1971–1973   Supervisory Mathematician, Department of the
Navy, USA

1967–1971   Mathematician, Department of the Navy, USA

1966–1967   President, Morehouse College Glee Club, Atlanta,
Georgia

1962–1963   President, Student Government Association, S.H.
Archer High School, Atlanta, Georgia

APPENDIX B

Awards and Honors

1996   Horatio Alger Award
Washington, D.C.

Metropolitan YMCA
Carl A. Nelson Award
Omaha, Nebraska

Jr. Achievement of Lincoln
Special Recognition
Lincoln, Nebraska

National Association of Health Underwriters
Spirit of Independence Award
Washington, D.C.

National Federation of Independent Business
Special Recognition
Lincoln, Nebraska

Nestle U.S.A.
Inclusion in "Men of Courage II"

Nation's Restaurant News
Hall of Fame
New York, New York

Penn State University
Conti Professor
University Park, Pennsylvania

Member of The National Commission
on Economic Growth and Tax Reform
Washington, D.C.

1995   Inductee: Hospitality Hall of Fame
Omaha, Nebraska

Distinguished Visiting Professor
Johnson & Wales University
Providence, Rhode Island

Certificate of Thanks
Nebraskans for Quality Health Care
Lincoln, Nebraska

Resolution of Gratitude
Creighton University Board of Directors
Omaha, Nebraska

Freedom Fighter Award
Lancaster Country Republican Party
Lincoln, Nebraska

Omaha Small Business Network, Inc.
Premier Fast Track Entrepreneurial Training Program
Omaha, Nebraska

Distinguished Service Award
Missouri Restaurant Association
Kansas City, Missouri

Dr. Geil M. Browning Award
Career Excellence & Community Involvement
Omaha, Nebraska

Certificate of Distinguished Service
Nebraska Restaurant Association
Lincoln, Nebraska

Sincere Appreciation as President of NRA
New Mexico Restaurant Association
Albuquerque, New Mexico

African American Award
Corporate and Community Leader
The Western Heritage Museum

"Profiles of Power"
(50 influential people in the restaurant industry)
Nation's Restaurant News

Special Recognition
Ak-Sar-Ben Court of Honor
Business & Industry
Omaha, Nebraska

1994   Omahan of the Year Award
Rotary Club of Omaha—Suburban
Omaha, Nebraska

Jefferson Award
American Institute for Public Service
KETV
Omaha, Nebraska

Humanitarian Award
National Conference of Christians & Jews
Omaha, Nebraska

1993   Distinguished Guest Lecturer
Cornell University, The Hotel School
Ithaca, New York

Distinguished Lecturer
Kansas State University, College of Business Administration
Manhattan, Kansas

1992   Foodservice Management Professional
Educational Foundation
National Restaurant Association
Chicago, Illinois

Advisory Board
People's Natural Gas
Omaha, Nebraska

Recognition Award
Minority Business Development Council
Dallas/Fort Worth, Texas

Special Recognition
National Black MBA Assoc., Inc.
St. Louis, Missouri

Special Recognition
DECCA—Central High School
Omaha, Nebraska

Special Recognition
MUFSO
Dallas, Texas

1991   Food Service Operator of the Year—Gold Plate Award
        International Food Manufacturers Association (IFMA)
        Chicago, Illinois

        Outstanding Contribution
        Sixth Nebraska Conference on Productivity and Enterprise
        Lincoln, Nebraska

        Gold Plate Award
        IFMA
        Chicago, Illinois

        Certificate of Lifetime Membership
        NAACP—Omaha Chapter
        Omaha, Nebraska

        Nebraska Small Business Associate of the Year
        U.S. Small Business
        Omaha, Nebraska

        Special Recognition
        Morton Jr. High School
        Omaha, Nebraska

        Outstanding Contribution
        Valuing Diversity Television Broadcast
        Marriott Corporation and Marriott Family Foundation
        Philadelphia, PA

        Distinguished Service Award
        All High School 20 Reunion (1971)
        Omaha, Nebraska

1990   Black Achiever in Business and Industry Award
        North YMCA
        Omaha, Nebraska

Entrepreneur of the Year
University of Nebraska - Lincoln
College of Business Administration

The Business Excellence Achievement Award
University of Nebraska—Lincoln
College of Business Administration

Outstanding Achievement & Leadership
Black DP Associates of Indianapolis
Indianapolis, Indiana

1989   Special Recognition
MUFSO
Nation's Restaurant News
New Orleans, Louisiana

Booker T. Washington Symbol of Service Award
National Business League
Birmingham, Alabama

High Business Achievements and Excellence
Civic Service
Frontiers, Inc.
Omaha, Nebraska

1988   Honors
Nebraska Black Manager's Association
Omaha, Nebraska

Professional Achievement Award
Morehouse College National Alumni Association
Atlanta, Georgia

Life Member Society
The Urban League of Nebraska
Omaha, Nebraska

National Prominence Award
The Urban League of Nebraska
Omaha, Nebraska

1987   MUFSO Golden Chain Award
        Nation's Restaurant News
        Los Angeles, California

1986   High Achievement Award
        Hospitality Management Program
        Bethune Cookman College
        Daytona Beach, Florida

1984   Symbol of Excellence
        Pillsbury Corporation
        Minneapolis, Minnesota

APPENDIX C

References

Glen L. Urban and Steven H. Star. *Advanced Marketing Strategy.*
   Englewood Cliffs, New Jersey: Prentice Hall, 1991.

Benjamin E. Mays. *Born To Rebel.*
   New York: Charles Scribner's Sons, 1971.

James M. Kouzes and Barry Z. Posner. *Credibility.*
   San Francisco: Jossey-Bass Inc., 1993.

Donald T. Phillips. *Lincoln On Leadership.*
   New York: Warner Books, 1992.

Al Ries and Jack Trout. *Marketing Warfare.*
   New York: McGraw Hill Publishers, 1986.

Dr. Robert Schuller. *Move Ahead With Possibility Thinking.*
   New York: Doubleday, 1967.

Colin Powell. *My American Journey.*
   New York: Random House, 1995.

"Restaurants USA," Interview by Elaine Graham.
   National Restaurant Association, January 1995.

Newt Gingrich. *To Renew America.*
   New York: Harper Collins, 1995.

Wall Street Journal, April 15, 1994.

INDEX

C

Herman Cain keynote speaking
video and audio tapes available.

For information contact:

T.H.E., Inc.
P.O. Box 540400
Omaha, NE 68154
(800) 698-2246